MADAM BESSIE JONES

HER LIFE AND TIMES

J. M. WEST

LOCAL HISTORY
PRESS

an imprint of Sunbury Press, Inc.
Mechanicsburg, PA USA

an imprint of Sunbury Press, Inc.
Mechanicsburg, PA USA

For information about special discounts for bulk purchases, please contact Sunbury Press Orders Dept. at (855) 338-8359 or orders@sunburypress.com.

To request one of our authors for speaking engagements or book signings, please contact Sunbury Press Publicity Dept. at publicity@sunburypress.com.

FIRST LOCAL HISTORY PRESS EDITION: April 2021

Set in Adobe Garamond | Interior design by Crystal Devine | Cover by Lawrence Knorr | Edited by Lawrence Knorr.

Publisher's Cataloging-in-Publication Data
Names: West, J. M., author.
Title: Madam Bessie Jones : her life and times / J. M. West.
Description: First trade paperback edition. | Mechanicsburg, PA : Local History Press, 2021.
Summary: Madam Bessie Jones's brothel in Carlisle, Pennsylvania, was in business from the 1920s to the 1970s, ending with her untimely death.
Identifiers: ISBN : 978-1-62006-537-2 (softcover).
Subjects: HISTORY / United States / State & Local / Middle Atlantic | HISTORY / Women | HISTORY / United States / 20th Century.

Product of the United States of America
0 1 1 2 3 5 8 13 21 34 55

Continue the Enlightenment!

Dedicated to:

The marginalized, outsiders, women, and children

————

Inspired, in part, by Langston's Hughes's poem
"Mother to Son"

This text is based upon historical fact and actual anecdotes about Black Carlisle citizens who created a business that contributed to the growth of the town and care of its African American community while catering to an elite White clientele. Although some historians have omitted them completely, I depict actual sites, landmarks, and historical events, and public persons in the context of the narrative. While I juggled a bit of the chronology, specifically the Fair, I did not alter the facts.

CONTENTS

FOREWORD

"CARLISLE MADAM MURDERED" shrieked the October 1972 *Sentinel* banner. An assailant gagged and tied Madam Bessie Jane Jones in her upstairs bedroom during a robbery. The killer knifed the 77-year-old-woman three times, one stab severing the pulmonary artery; she bled out.

Detective Robert Warner presided over the crime scene and the case. An officer found the murder weapon, a four-inch switch-blade, in the yard with traces of the victim's blood. Prostitute Georgia Ann Schneider fled the premises in a taxi with $2,789 stuffed into her clothes; Officer Mike Brennen stopped the taxi on the Pennsylvania Turnpike and detained the suspect at the Newville Substation for robbery and fleeing a crime scene. The District Attorney later arrested and charged the pregnant White woman with the murder.

About 4:30 A.M. the morning of the crime, another call girl called police from the Star Lite Motel to report her failure to gain admittance to 20 East Locust Street residence known as "Bessie's House." Cassandra Jackson later appeared as the star witness for the prosecution at the Schneider's February 11, 1973, trial.[1]

Most locals know the basics of Bessie Jane Jones's murder. The woman had run a lucrative brothel or "house of ill repute" for fifty years, as had her mother Cora Andrews before her. Two books— Paul Zdinak's *Bessie's House* and Joe Cress's *Wicked Carlisle*—as well as numerous newspaper accounts—provide salacious details of the gruesome killing, the trial, and the defendant's subsequent acquittal forty-seven years ago. Yet mysteries like who killed Madam Jones remain.

My goal here is to peer into the morass, revisit the scenes, and ask the questions participants glossed over from 1972 to 1973 and offer a more complete picture of Bessie Jones. In the 1990s, *The Sentinel* ran an article that Schneider's defense attorney had Jones's "sex book" locked away in a safe. The murder resurfaced recently in a *Sunday Patriot New* article and on a PennLive video in which Herbert ("Corky") Goldstein reenacted his closing argument; the jury acquitted his client of murder.

Because the book is out of print, I summarize key observations and testimony in Zdinak's *Bessie's House*. The title is a misnomer; it should be titled *Georgia Ann Schneider's Journey*, or maybe *Georgia Ann's Descent* or *Fall from Grace* since the bulk of the book describes the girl's marriage, birth of a son, entry into prostitution at eighteen, sojourn in New York, and then work at Bessie's. More valuable is part of the trial transcript—a first-hand witness to history. Though the author summarized the defense strategy well, he implied the Prosecution lacked convincing or concrete evidence. The jury agreed.

Second, *Bessie's House* contains inaccurate and conflicting information. For example, Zdinak states that David Andrews was her husband. However, Cora Andrews's (Bessie's mother) death notice reported her as the daughter of Jane and David Andrews. Other sources, including the 1900 Census, report that Andrews was a single mother.

Journalist Joseph D. Cress's two chapters in *Wicked Carlisle* on Cora Andrews and Madam Bessie Jones offer more accurate information on this material, citing the raids and arrests of mother and daughter, the burglaries, arson, and downfall of the famous madam. I use the term 'famous' rather than 'notorious' or' infamous' because, ironically, Carlisle citizens greeted "Miss Bessie" on the streets, knew she attended the Presbyterian Church, and regarded her as a 'Black businesswoman'—no small feat in 1922, when in her twenties, Jones replaced her mother as Madam of the household.

A colorful anecdote claims that Jane Andrews, Jones's grandmother, traveled north to Carlisle with the Confederate Army as a "comfort woman." I found no evidence her grandmother engaged in prostitution. The legend adds a bit of spice with an undercurrent of spite because this idea objectifies women, Blacks, and prostitutes.

The 1860 Census refutes the legend; it records the family as living in Carlisle; all Jane Andrews's children were born in Carlisle. The tale also begs the question why would a free Black travel South during the Civil War and run the danger of being captured and forced into slavery? No sensible woman would take such a risk.

At times, historical records about Madam Jones conflict with one another. Jones's birth date is listed as 1895 on her headstone but 1899 elsewhere. Four children accompanied Andrews to court and the Cumberland County Jail in 1899 when she was arrested. The court then sent the children to the hospital, deeming the jail unsuitable for young children. Albert, fifteen, the eldest, preceded William and Bessie. They were likely twins (or possibly nine-eleven months apart) at eleven years old, followed by Marion, five, and Vermont four in the 1900 Census. So, I conclude the headstone is correct.

As adults, both of Jones's sisters, Marion Gibson/Middleton, and Vermont Brown, married and lived down the street at 24 Locust Street at various times. At one point, Bessie's husband resided with her briefly. Some records indicate he died; another said the couple divorced. Where conflicting facts occur, I've included both.

Most of the town's citizens tolerated the presence of Cora's House; others detested it—gossip ran like a virus, and still, others ignored it. Perhaps some did not know of her. One disgruntled citizen, Dickinson College President George Reed, "lodged a complaint and filed charges against Cora Andrews about the immoral influence of the cathouse as a blight on Carlisle's good name."[2] Another complained of the noise—a fight in the alley between Andrews and a neighbor.

At any rate, questions beg answers. My thesis will flesh out Miss Bessie's life and illustrate that her contributions and success stem from shrewd assessment of her environment, status, and situation. She operated an illegal brothel three blocks from the police station for fifty years with only occasional raids, arrests, fines, and one protracted prison sentence at Muncy State Prison, another visit the next year, and a short stint in a federal pen in Virginia. News sources and authors report her strict rules of denying students and Blacks admission to the premises, keeping a low profile, and providing a service to an elite Caucasian clientele; these factors kept law enforcement from closing her doors until the last decade of her life.[3]

During one court appearance, Jones's attorney, Hyman "Hymie" Goldstein, described "Bessie's Place" as a "venerable institution comparable to Jim Thorpe and Molly Pitcher." That comment raised eyebrows, but her lawyer asserted that Bessie was a decent person who kept a clean and ordered establishment.[4]

Questions remain about her demise. What information was withheld or omitted from the trial? Why did the defendant's lawyer allegedly destroy Jones's Preference and Receipt books? They contained damning lists of men who frequented "Bessie's Place," their preferred sexual appetites, and what they paid for assignations with prostitutes. If admitted as evidence, these books could have pointed to motive and contain suspects. Why did the

District Attorney say the books were not relevant information? The killer could have been among the Madam's "high-class" clientele! The ledgers were destroyed to protect the names of those lawyers, judges, police, and the legislators who frequented Bessie's! On the other hand, men could have used aliases, but most did not know Jones kept records.

This book will address other questions as the situations surface from the murky fog of the past, including why Bessie's case remains unsolved to this day, although former Judge Mike Eakin claims he had the right culprit, and current D.A. Skip Ebert has no plans to reopen the case.[5]

Besides written and online accounts, I relied on personal interviews and observations, as well as individuals who shared anecdotes, The Cumberland County Historical Society, and journalist/author Pat LaMarche. I have reconstructed dialogue from testimony, records, and interviews and 'stood in Jones's shoes' to intuit her thoughts and reactions. To provide a context for Bessie's time, I've skimmed through relevant historical highlights.

PROLOGUE

March 1959

"Don't look. Don't look! Don't look!" ordered the owner of the Carlisle Hardware as he turned his daughters, five and fifteen, away from the window and shepherded them to the back of the store. "Get your satchels—time for school."

They'd looked and seen two prostitutes—one redhead and one blonde—swinging hatboxes and waiting at the bus stop for the ride to Harrisburg. Painted with eye-make-up and rouge, one wore a sweater under a fitted jacket, white pedal pushers, and high-heels, despite the frigid weather. The other one tugged at her tight black skirt, looking up and down the street for the bus.

"Glad to be shut of that place. It's a dump," said the redhead.

"You're not saying that because we got busted and jailed?"

"Nah, bet that's a first for you!"

The younger woman nodded. "That was scary! Gotta say, though, I've been in worse places. At least we're not walking the streets. I feel safe at Bessie's. We have a real bed, good food, and a clean house, even if it's a bit shabby."

"We're making her money, so she could afford to spruce up the place."

"She's keeping a low profile. I ain't got any complaints; she pays for our physicals." The younger one continued. "And buys all our supplies like new lingerie, sponges, vinegar, and condoms.

And soap, Listerine, and Lysol. Fixes our meals. Who else does that? She's doin' her best—gettin' the concrete porch repaired."

"But she charges room and board, and she's awfully demanding." The redheaded woman motioned down the road. Shifting from one foot to the other, she cracked her gum. "And bossy. And all her rules are ridiculous!"

"The rules protect us. And she screens the johns. Keeps out the riffraff. I'll take that over a beating from a street pick-up any day! I've suffered a few beatings from drunk dicks. When are we due back?"

"Steve rotates us in pairs; now we're on to New Kensington, Philly, and Pittsburgh, maybe another—unless we want to strike out for Baltimore or New York. So, in two months."

"No, I'd rather stay in Pennsylvania."

Finally, the bus lumbered to the corner of Hanover and Locust Street and wheezed to a stop. They climbed on, relieved to leave Carlisle and the scrutiny of its inhabitants.

The duo had walked from 20 East Locust Street—an alley, really, down a block or so. The dilapidated, two-and-a-half-story grey slate house had seen better days. A burn scarred the right side; crumbling concrete led to a covered porch with ivy climbing up one side. Once white, a dirty lattice wall left of the door guarded the house from prying eyes. A weathered front door stood sentinel beside two curtain-covered windows. Masking tape held the screen in place on the second window. Shades masked what lay behind the upstairs windows.

Inside, a kitchen with chipped Formica counters and mismatched chairs occupied the middle; worn appliances and cabinets lined the wall while the "parlor" was outfitted with a linoleum floor and record player with forty-fives stacked on the spindle for dancing. When on duty, the girls lounged in slinky lingerie that accentuated their assets. Upstairs they served the johns in the

Bessie's house. (Courtesy of the Cumberland County Historical Society.)

two back bedrooms; the front bedroom belonged to Bessie with the bathroom next door. The girls slept in the attic—sweltering during the summer and freezing in winter.

Carlisle citizens knew about Bessie's Place, where well-heeled White gentlemen who could afford the $10 for straight sex, slam-bam, pay the ma'am; $15 for half and half (intercourse and oral sex) or extra bucks for other, more daring predilections. Most men came attired in white dress shirts and suits—judges, lawyers, doctors, police, soldiers, congressmen, and others—all named in the madam's preference book with preferred acts and money paid for services. According to her lawyer, Hyman Goldstein, Bessie ran a fine establishment—'a venerable institution' he compared to Molly Pitcher and Jim Thorpe.[6]

CHAPTER 1

WHY PROSTITUTES HERE?

Why did a house of prostitution not only exist but also thrive in downtown Carlisle, a historical community, the county seat, and a bastion of rural, conservative, Republican-dominated citizenry—home to The Carlisle Indian Industrial School (until its closing in 1918), Dickinson College and Law Schools, the Carlisle Barracks and Olympic athlete Jim Thorpe. The town is also the burial site of the renowned Revolutionary War heroine Mary Ludwig Hayes MacCully (aka Molly Pitcher) and Madam Bessie Jane Jones.

Several reasons for the brothel's success come to mind: a productive, changing, and mobile workforce and religious and social conventions. Men could engage in unencumbered sex free from baggage or conditions; they could control and rebel against the status quo. They could unwind in fantasies, engage in more exciting sex than with the weary wife at home, burdened with domestic responsibilities. Men who frequented cathouses may have been lonely or subconsciously fixated on the Madonna/whore complex—where the wife, if a virgin, represented the former and the prostitute, the latter, the forbidden fruit.

Between 1900 and 1910, African Americans migrated from the South to Pennsylvania and other northern cities seeking jobs, then again during both World Wars when the United States cut

European immigration. During the Great Depression, the unemployment rate rose to double digits; commerce came to a sudden halt on Black Tuesday, October 29, 1929, when the stock market crashed. No industry, no jobs, no money, so no purchases translated to a life of misery and hardship that affected Carlisle—like the rest of the nation.

When the United States entered World War II, Pennsylvania rebounded to full employment—partly because of the high military presence in the area: the Carlisle Barracks, Mechanicsburg Naval Depot, Fort Indiantown Gap, and Letterkenny Depot in Chambersburg. The shoe, clothing, dry goods, drug, machine, laundry, carpet, and businesses like Frog and Switch needed workers. New ones like the Standard Piezo Company needed three shifts of workers to make crystals for radios for the Army. For the town's size, Carlisle attracted industry, thrived, and contained the workforce that patronized Bessie's Place.

The citizens seemed conservative, religious, somber, steadfast, law-abiding, responsible, hardworking, and community minded. The town boasted more than twenty churches. Quakers, pacifists who tolerated other religious sects, settled Penn's Wood, so Catholics and Protestants of all denominations flocked to the area.

Also, we still consider ours a Puritan, patriarchal nation; women have been sexually repressed for centuries—harshly rebuked for pre-marital sex and expected to move from their father's houses to their husband's a virgin. Those who behaved outside the boundaries of societal expectations were severely punished. Literary examples abound: Mary Magdalene, Chaucer's "The Miller's Tale," Shakespeare's Gertrude and Ophelia in *Hamlet*, Hawthorne's Hester *Scarlet Letter,* Hardy's Tess, and D. H. Lawrence's *Lady Chatterley's Lover*, et al.

Therefore, reasonable people can assume that traditional wives might balk at their husbands' marital demands and refuse sex that deviated from procreation. We have a history of the social acceptance of politicians, celebrities, and professional athletes engaging with "loose" women. For whatever reason, men came to this brothel for nearly a century. First, Cora Andrews, then Madam Bessie Jones, provided prostitutes and their services in a warm, clean, and friendly environment.

However, along with migration and resettlement, resentment and prejudice rode along. Ethnocentrism, prejudice, and even racism seem *sui generi* in America, slavery being the primary reason leading to the Civil War, but the economy played a major role. The North had the advantage of industry, while the South produced mostly cotton and tobacco, which required many hands to till and toil. Factors like states' rights versus the powers of the Federal government also caused heated debate. While too complex to analyze here, the Civil War created a deep divide among American citizens that resonates even today. Finally, Carlisle harbored "Southern sympathizers, which became a hotbed for White supremacists . . . with the rise of the Ku Klux Klan in the 1910s."[7] So, a Black madam who catered only to Caucasian men would suit the clan's notions of social order.

From the 1920s on, the KKK in Carlisle advocated White supremacy while intimidating Blacks, Catholics, and Jews. Nationally, racial tensions simmered up through the fifties and sixties until the Supreme Court in *Brown vs. Board of Education* struck down the 1896 "separate but equal" legislation—effectively beginning the march toward Civil Rights. Rosa Parks' refusal to surrender her bus seat, federal troops forcing Little Rock, Arkansas, to integrate, and Dr. Martin Luther's King's leadership, urging non-violent civil disobedience—kindled a struggle with disparities still evident today.

Also, schools and churches were segregated in Carlisle until 1947. Before that, the Ladies Benevolent Society held classes for Black students in the A.M.E. church basement on East Pomfret Street, and nuns offered classes, kindergarten through eighth grades, across the street at St. Patrick's Church.[8]

Another sign of prejudice: African-Americans had to use the balcony at the Comfort or Strand Theater (Orpheum in the 1920s), but children thought, "That's the way it was. We didn't consider it racism."[9] But any institution, entity, or organization that diminishes, isolates, discriminates, or deprives others of their rights *is* racism. Owning and admitting our past might open a meaningful dialogue among our citizens.

From time to time, locals would voice their complaints at having a brothel in their midst. Irate wives might call the police and demand the brothel be closed, especially if the husband spent his paycheck at Bessie's and returned home empty-handed. Police would raid "Bessie's Place," arrest and occasionally drag the prostitutes to jail. The judges would typically fine Jones and charge her for court costs but release the men without charges.

Pastors preached from their pulpits. The righteous flung their arrows of judgment, the gossips' tongues wagged, and men leered at the prostitutes when they walked by. The Black community didn't talk much about Bessie's, according to one Black historian. Despite numerous arrests, lectures, fines, and court appearances, "Bessie's House" continued to serve its customers.

CHAPTER 2

THE ANDREWS GIRLS

Within this context, Jane Andrews and her family had lived in Carlisle since 1860, listing her children: Charles, 6; David, 2; and Cora, four months.[10] No other records trace the family's movements until her only daughter became a teen.

Cora Andrews, a single mother, had her first child at sixteen. According to the U.S. 1900 Census, Cora Andrews lived in Carlisle, Pennsylvania, Ward 1, at Mulberry Lane, Cumberland County with her children: Albert (Ahl), 15; Willie and Bessie, 11; Marion, 5; and Vermont Andrews, 4.[11] If we do the math, they were all were older than other records indicate. We know little about them as children, save for one reference that a son, caught between and wagon wheel and a tree, needed twenty stitches to close his scalp.[12] As adults, we learn only what we read in books, newspapers and hear from anecdotes. At one point, their mother published announcements in *The Sentinel* that she would not pay for Marion Andrews's debts or Albert Ahl's tab for alcohol consumption.[13]

Perhaps she turned to "running a bawdy house" as one of the few occupations where a single Black woman could support herself and her children—compared to her income as a Madam, working as a domestic, waitress, or toiling at a factory job paid a mere pittance.

Cora, however, ran "Cora's Place" discreetly, as far as records indicate, with a few exceptions. She deeded the East Locust Street house to her youngest daughter, Vermont, who—upon her early death—left her estate to her mother and siblings. Marion and Vermont lived two houses down at 24 East Locust and often joined their family for dinner. Assuming Bessie had other plans when she married William Jones, her name nevertheless appears in the November 5, 1917, arrest record.[14] Jones returned home after her husband's death or divorce and bought the house at 20 East Locust Street from her mother. Cora Andrews retires but continues to assist, as arrest records attest. Despite the odds, Cora and Bessie's business survived the Great War, the 1918 flu epidemic, Prohibition, and the growth of urbanization.

From 1917 through the 1920s, Carlisle expanded, issuing 240 building permits in that year alone, and thriving businesses included W.C. Clarke's bookstore, Dutrey's Shoes, Horn's Drug-store, Robbin's Florist, George's Flowers, the Ewing Brothers Funeral Home, Kronenberg's, and Bowman Department Stores, among others.[15]

Henry Ford, Thomas A. Edison, Alexander Graham Bell, and hundreds of other inventors, backed by J.P. Morgan, R.D. Rock-efeller, Andrew Carnegie, and Andrew Mellon's millions, helped technology and invention steamroll across the nation. Carlisle prospered and grew. From World War I through World War II, the radio brought mass communication.[16] Frank W. Woolworth introduced the first successful five-and-dime store where working people could finally afford household items, followed by others like Kresge's and Murphy's.

Only the affluent could afford Model Ts, but by the 1930s in Carlisle, they jostled for road space with the horse-drawn carriages. If Ford initiated American mobility, then the radio brought the world to Carlisle: news, music, and entertainment.

At the time, jazz dominated the airwaves. Singers, writers, poets, and musicians like Louis Armstrong, Langston Hughes, Duke Ellington (et al.), and later Count Basie, Billie Holiday, Sarah Vaughn, and Charlie Parker converged at the Cotton Club during the Harlem Renaissance and beyond.

In the 1950s, Nat King Cole, Marion Anderson, and Dinah Washington became popular. Another sensation that merged rhythm and blues burst onto the musical stage; the fans dubbed him "the King" of rock and roll. With the advent of rock and roll combined with rhythm and blues, singers like Johnny Mathis, Harry Bellefonte, and Mary Wells became popular. Bands like the Platters, Little Anthony and the Imperials, Diana Ross and the Supremes, The Righteous Brothers, Frankie Valli and the Four Seasons, The Four Tops, and a host of others exploded during the fifties and sixties. The invasion of the Beatles, Rolling Stones, Animals, and other British bands added their talents to the airwaves.*

As the years peeled past, Bessie's Place enjoyed a steady stream of business. The decades rolled by in a chain of mild and volatile seasons witnessing wars, disease, including the pandemic called the Spanish flu, change and upheaval of the Roaring Twenties to the turbulent Sixties. In total, Bessie's business spanned fifty years—from Woodrow Wilson's presidency through Richard Nixon's.

---

* The singers listed are representative of their times; it is not intended to be a definitive list.

CHAPTER 3

PASSING THE TORCH

November 1917

After dodging both horse-drawn carriages and the new-fangled, noisy motorcars coughing along Main Street, Bessie stepped over the trolly rails, which could be slick when wet or cold. She turned down East Locust Street, strode into the house, and stacked the bills in front of her mother. Perspiration dotted her forehead. Without preamble, she asked, "Why you gonna charge me if you're gonna deed Vermont the house?"

"I'm not yet. She too young, but eventually, we need to keep it safe. If the house be in her name, the government can't take it. You're buying the business. It worth more, an' it's our living. Runnin' it is important. Just look how hard it is keeping the place clean 'n tidy, time the girls' schedules, fixin' meals and keeping the books.

"My life 'ain't been no highway to heaven.' I work hard to keep it goin', but I'm getting weary. My joints ache 'n my chilblains actin' up. I kin still keep the budget and pay for the liquor. And work the New Kensington angle." Cora pushed the pile of cash toward her daughter. "We can wait 'till you're ready, but you my oldest girl and the most responsible. Marion spends too much money. Vermont's not able."

"What New Kensington angle?" Bessie slipped out of her black heels. She looked at the cash.

"The girls come from Pittsburgh, Philadelphia, and Baltimore, sometimes Reading, but I got a man from New Kensington who handles their schedules and transportation."

"I thought they rode the bus from Harrisburg," Bessie answered.

"That too. I can still make arrangements. You run the day-to-day part."

"OK. When I buy the business, I'm making changes. First—no students—not from the Indian School either." She shifted her weight.

"Why? They pays their money, aren't rowdy like those frat boys—"

"Because they're students!" Bessie emphasized. "They draw too much attention from the cops. And I'm not turning tricks anymore Just goin' t'be the Madam."

"Why not?"

"'Cause I'm married."

"Your husband doesn't know?" Cora asked.

Bessie shook her head. "That's not it. I don't think he's comfortable staying here. We'll live on Post. I'll hire another girl. And no more admitting strangers. It's too risky 'cause they could be cops or plants. New customers'll need another john to vouch for 'em or a give a password." However, Fate decreed Bessie's husband, William Jones, did not return to Carlisle; either he died, or the couple separated or obtained a divorce. So, she stayed at 20 East Locust Street.

"OK. That reasonable. No need to be 'shamed, Bess. It's our livelihood."

"I'm not, but people stare and talk."

"And they always will. We're Black women running an illegal business in a conservative town. You got to 'cept that. That's the

9

only way I raised five chillun, put food in your mouths, clothes on your backs, and a roof over your heads.

"Just don't draw attention; mind your manners, and nod when people say 'Good afternoon' on the streets. Nothing else. And if'n you get dragged to court, admit we run a bawdy house, pay the fines, and keep calm. Keep a low profile in town." Andrews lit the parlor lamps; the gold flames flickered and held. Their shadows ghosted against the faded wallpaper as darkness smothered the light.

"Then we wait." Bessie collected the pile of bills, rushed upstairs, and stuffed her savings in her bedroom's hiding place. Stripping off her street clothes, she slid a kimono over her underwear and slipped downstairs.

Door knocking signaled the arrival of johns. Gay Newman and Marion adjusted their sheer negligees and perched on the sofa. Cora admitted the soldiers and two civilians and then moved to the kitchen to bring out the Jack Daniels and bottles of beer. She took their orders, charging a quarter a shot or a bottle. Bessie put a thirty-three record on the Victrola. "Let's dance!" The taller one removed his shirt; his t-shirt stretched across firm muscles.

Warming up, two locals grabbed Gay and Marion, danced them to the stairwell, and followed them up. The soldiers waited their turns, content to boogie to the "St. Louis Blues."

"What's that music called?" asked the fellow with black hair shorn into a buzz cut and blue eyes shuffling along, his eyes on Bessie's feet.

"Jazz. Ain't it grand? It's based on improvisin' three sets of chords, starting with middle "C" as one, then striking every other one: three, five, and sometime seven. Move up an octave, play every other note. I could show you if we had a piano." Bessie played her fingers along an imaginary scale on his chest.

"Sounds complicated," he said. "Do you play?"

"Not really. Didn't you have music in school?" She returned.

"A choir. We sang Handel's 'Messiah' at Christmas. Alleluia! Alleluia!" he sang in a decent baritone. He moved in against her, his hands sliding down her backside.

"Not bad! What's your name, soldier?" Bessie asked.

"Sean O'Brien. What tipped you off? The haircut?" He pulled her in and turned her around.

"Uh-huh. What'd you do? Isn't the war nearly over?" she asked.

"Not by a long shot. We've got a lot of mopping up to do yet. The Krauts leveled France and bombed England, perty near destroyed everything; we have to help rebuild. And the winds of war are blowing again. Bet another one's coming. Germany's still gonna be a thorn in our side."

"Oh, no. Don't say that!" Bessie said. "You'll jinx us for sure!"

"Why? It's human nature. Men are violent creatures who'd rather fight for freedom than give in to a tyrant."

"You've heard of 'flight or fight' when you're cornered?" Another soldier with dirty blonde hair and acne scars pocking his cheeks wore an olive sweater over pleated khaki slacks. Shot glass in hand, he stood by the banister waiting. "We fight! The Krauts sank the *Lusitania* back in '15—they attacked civilians, killing more than a hundred Americans and our allies. We had to retaliate!"

"It's just awful scary. *The Sentinel* writes articles 'bout German submarines sneaking along our coast," Bessie commented. "They glide underwater, waiting to attack our boats. To change the subject, Bessie offered, "Have another drink," pointing them to the kitchen. "I have to run to the necessary!" The clock struck eleven.

"So, either we fight or die anyway. Don't want my kids speaking Ger—"

One of the local guys interrupted, following Gay back downstairs. "Something smells mighty good."

"Come on. Chicken and waffles 'r ready." Cora smiled. "Sit. Eat."

Bessie glanced out the upstairs window and then shuddered as a long, grey touring car slinked up alongside the curb with two police cars right behind it, cops perched on the running boards. She cracked the window open. "Who's there?" she called out. Then came pounding on the door. But she saw the Man. She rapped hard at Gay and Marion's doors. "Cops!" Her heart pulsed in her neck; her palms grew sweaty as she ran down the stairs to the front door envisioning handcuffs and iron bars. Fanning her face, she coached, "Oh, no. Stay calm. Mama will handle this." Bessie Jones had never been arrested before.

"Open up, or we'll break it down," ordered the policeman. The rear door caved in as Bessie unlocked the front door. "We're eating our dinner."

"This is a police raid. We're arresting everyone on the premises and taking you downtown. Come along. You ladies should get dressed first," one officer remarked. They waited while Gay, Marion, and Bessie slipped into street clothes, donned their coats, hats, and grabbed their purses.

In court, District Attorney George Lloyd charged Cora Andrews for "operating a bawdy house." She paid the $1000 fine and court costs for her and Bessie. Andrews then spent a few days in the imposing Cumberland County Jail[17] that looked and felt more like a medieval stone fortress. Drafts whistled through gaps in the windows; cold and damp of years seeped through the stone. Watching a spider ladder up her web and wind the captured moth like a mummy, she shivered, wrapped her coat around her, and lay her body down.

Charged with "violating the criminal code," Marion and Gay paid their $50 fine and returned to 20 East Locust Street after spending a few hours in the courthouse jail.

Surprisingly, the police questioned and released the soldiers from the 59th Infantry stationed in Gettysburg and the "Carlislers" caught in the dragnet. The lawmen confiscated 100 bottles of beer and whiskey from the premises. Rather than waste the liquor, the judge sent it to Carlisle Hospital at Claremont Farms for 'medicinal purposes.' "What effect the raid will have on the morals of this town remains to be seen . . . [D]ecent citizens hope for the sake of the town that the Andrews place has been eradicated forever"[18]

They hoped in vain. "Bessie's Place" thrived for fifty-five more years because the owner knew her community: barring her door to Black men and students while catering to an elite, White clientele translated to less attention and interference from the law.[18] Both she and her mother kept a low profile, maintained the business, admitting only regulars or men whom steady customers referred. Besides, a church-going woman, Bessie kept a tight rein on 'her girls,' as she called the prostitutes.

Miss Bessie had rules for the girls: keep their rooms and themselves clean and stay indoors dressed for work; wash the sheets every day; go for a physical annually and wash the patrons' privates before they engage in sex. Always use rubbers.

She assigned them chores like doing dishes, helping with the laundry, sweeping the stoop, and cleaning the bathroom but later hired a maid, Beatrice Ahl, to help her with the housekeeping, marketing, and running errands. Together they strolled along the stands at the farmer's market, buying fresh produce, eggs, and meat. Every week, Jones would purchase fresh fragrant flowers—gladiolas in spring or mums in the fall to brighten her home and lighten her mood.

CHAPTER 4

DEJA VU

A year later, on November 2, 1918, the scene repeated; on this night, the girls, Cora, Bessie, Marion, and Gay, were again enjoying a chicken and waffle dinner with four soldiers and two men.[19]

"We're lucky to've survived that war,' The tall, lanky soldier said; he tugged off his facemask that tossed heated breath back onto his face despite the autumn chill. Stuffed it in his pants' pocket. "Better to be a pilot and buy the farm rather than the infantry dying in the trenches."

His companion's mask disappeared in his cap; he swiped a hand across his crewcut. He grunted in disbelief, reaching inside his front pocket for a cigarette, tucked it over his ear. "I'm shocked we survived the war. The Krauts used deadly mustard and chlorine gases and who knows what else to poison us?

"The trenches offered little protection. When it rained, we were mired in mud; try climbing out of a slippery trench carrying a rifle with a bayonet, gas mask flopping on your belt. If you breathed in the gas—too late. Goner, for sure.

"They mowed us down with Panzer tanks; we were sitting ducks! A living Hell, believe me. And then came the galdang flu to finish us off!"

"Galdang?" his companion remarked.

"Don' want to swear around the ladies."

14

The girls twittered at that remark.

"Newspapermen claim soldiers brought—some say the Asian flu, others, Spanish—back to the states; I reckon we did." The tall soldier who limped from an injury continued. "Yeah. Bodies piled up in the big cities." He shuddered. "In the trenches, guys dropped like flies in three days: first came the fever, then coughs, chills, pneumonia . . . their lungs filled . . ." He snapped his fingers . . . "And then they died!"

"I'm from Boston originally—"

"Now stationed in Gettysburg," the guy with the buzz cut chimed in. "And the mayor closed schools, churches, and businesses 'cause so many died; the sanitation company closed; garbage pilled ten-foot-high in the streets; people were quarantined." Fifty thousand Americans died from the deadliest disease in its history, while approximately 48,000 died in battle.[20]

"Ain't even gonna mention the rats." The one with acne lit his cigarette and inhaled; smoke spiraled into the air with the tang of tobacco as he exhaled. "But with the World War, a pandemic, 'n' all, seems like Armageddon's upon us."

"We'll get through this. We wear masks when we go out, avoid crowds, and stay indoors mostly. We make camphor bag necklaces for us and the litte'uns and worry when they leave the house. Even hung them in the outhouse. When we go out, we risk getting the flu—maybe the air itself is infected! Most downtown businesses shut their doors. Carlisle's become a ghost town!" Bessie declared.

Vermont added, "We're so sorry. We tried to help on the home front, sending care packages overseas—collected scrap metal. And wrote you guys letters and sent care packages. Look at the Red Cross volunteers! You soldiers say that terrible flu killed more doughboys than the war, but now we've turned the corner,"

Vermont added. She stood up. "I have to go. My man is supposed to get home tomorrow. Thanks for dinner, mama."

The men stood as Vermont grabbed her coat and scurried down the alley.

"But it's worse over there?" asked Cora.

As they returned to their seats, one soldier remarked, "Oh, much worse. Cities reduced to rubble; grey, crumbling ruins wherever you look. Land and people shrouded in despair. Survivors scrounge for scarce food and clean water while they stare into space. Most lost all their possessions. Their animals were confiscated or killed. But they fought on. And, with allied reinforcements, turned the tide, by God."

"Thanks for supper, ma'am," the Carlisle john said. He sopped up the gravy with the last bite of waffle. "It's mighty good. Best meal I've had in ages."

The second civilian joined in, "Can't beat home-cooking. Thank you kindly, Mrs. Andrews."

Marion jumped up. "Oh, we ain't done. We got dessert yet."

"Who wants punkin' pie with ice cream?"

"Think I've died and gone to heaven!" claimed the fidgety one.

While clearing the dishes from the dining room table, Bessie could hear scratching at the back door. She laid two leftover waffles in the kitchen, sliced the leftover chicken and scooped collard greens into a tin pie pan, wrapped it in newspaper, and padded to the rear. A neighbor down the alley stood in the dark, his ragged coat shredding along the wrists. His bare hands shook from the frigid air. He accepted the tin of food.

"Thank you kindly, Miz Jones," he said. "Ain't found work yet. Carpet Mills not hiring. May have to move my family if I can't pay the rent."

"You're welcome, Ralph. Keep on looking. I hear Deckman & Sons need a couple men to load furniture into the moving van." She dug in her pocket and handed him a five-dollar bill. "And Troy Laundry needs a custodian."

"God bless you, Miz Jones." He shuffled away into the night.

"It's hard work, being poor," she said to the frosty air. "I know what it like goin' t'bed hungry and wearing church bazaar hand-me-downs. It's hard work scratching at the dirt or scraping pennies together for enough milk, cornmeal, eggs, and flour to make cornbread," she mumbled into the dark starless night. "Going barefoot to school and dividin' our food into six portions." Then Jones closed the door against the cold. The front door rattled.

"Police! This is a raid!" a voice yelled. "Open up!"

Andrews trudged to the door, sighing. "Why don't they go arrest a real criminal like a bootlegger? Or a mobster?"

The soldiers headed to the back door to escape, but the detective blocked the exit. "You're under arrest for aiding and abetting an illegal and immoral enterprise."

"Come on, officer. We just returned from the war; we're blowing off steam. A little dancing—we've done nothing illegal. Cut us a break." The lanky one blocked the doorway.

"I can smell the whiskey on your breath! Does Madam Andrews have a liquor license? Hands on your head, soldier." The uniform pushed into the room, muscling the veteran aside.

Police hauled everyone to the station and again *released* the men but arraigned the women, charging them with operating a house of ill repute and assignation.

"This is becoming a habit," Bessie muttered to Marion.

"Kinda like a stuck record," her sister remarked.

CHAPTER 5

CHANGING OF THE GUARD

On December 5, 1922, police thundered up to the door, barged in, and arrested the women at Cora's Place. This time, the judge sentenced Cora Andrews to a year in jail because the authorities had no knowledge of her turning the brothel over to Bessie, which may have been a mother's gesture to protect her daughter and the business. That same day, the court charged Louise Figueria, Gertrude Weaver, and Blanche G. Marzenello—all for keeping "bawdy houses"[21] in Pennsylvania and Maryland.

During the 1920s, the business and technology boom translated into a quiet decade for the Andrews family; police hauled Cora into court again for operating a house of ill repute, but otherwise, Carlisle bustled with business; the borough sold 91 building permits in 1922 for garages alone and more in the next two years, which points to the growing prosperity and popularity of the motorcar. Carlisle expanded: businessmen like J. Herman Bosler invested in the shoe industry and built the library. Robert R. Ford bought into the Plank Clothing Company and John Hays, who owned Frog and Switch, built spacious homes along Mooreland Avenue and College Street. The borough laid and paved streets, connecting the town to the annexed area, which added 137 acres to the town. Motorcars multiplied. Train tracks cut down the middle of High Street. The Hotel Carlisle, John S. Bursk's Hatter, Castle's Lumber, The Wagner Hardware Store, John Graybill Electric, and Dr. Beeteem, Chiropractor (et al.) opened for business.[22]

When Bessie finally bought the business, she and her sisters freshened the interior. They dusted, swept the floors, and beat the area rugs. New flowered curtains flapped at the windows; the sisters scrubbed the kitchen. Laid a new oilcloth on the table and washed the oil lamps. Marion pressed a lacey tablecloth on the dining room table and tidied the china cabinet. At the same time, they listened to Paul Robeson's "Old Man River" on their new Philco radio, setting on its stand in the parlor, *cum* living room.

A man pecked furtively at the back door—a liquor delivery, the bottles hidden in boxes. Prohibition outlawed producing, selling, and transporting liquor from 1920 to 1933. "Many Americans responded by opening speakeasies—private clubs—or distilling their own. To enforce the Volstead Act, President Hoover hired thousands of agents to pursue criminals caught bootlegging."[23] In Carlisle, Bessie's Place doubled as a speakeasy and bordello; men could cast off their cares, drink, dance and bed a girl.

Bessie tugged some bills from the coffee can and hastened to the back door. "Just set the boxes on the kitchen table." She doled out the dollars. "Thanks."

"Where's Cora?" The stranger asked, pocketing the money; his scruffy beard, rough shirt, and patched breeches gave off the odor of sweat, cigarettes, and hooch.

"She in jail." Bessie surveyed the bottles of Jack Daniels (The label read 'for medicinal purposes' only), near-beer, and several bottles of wine—an unlabeled red, muscatel, and a California white. "What are these?"

"Bootlegged. Hard to get the real thing."

"I'm paying good money. I want good wine, not some home-made hooch. Who knows what's in this stuff? And I don't want my clients going blind."

"It's real wine; it ain't like moonshine." He picked at his cuffs and waited by the back door.

"Get me real beer," she pushed the box of near beer back, "or my money back." She stowed the wine bottles in the kitchen cabinet and locked the door, smoothed down her apron as the man shuffled out with the near beer. The rest she carried to the basement.

He returned with a case labeled Anheuser Busch. "Malt and baker's yeast. You make your own."

Marion studied the directions on the box and said, "I can do this."

Vermont scrunched up her nose as the man stumbled out. Marion rolled her eyes at the stench of liquor, cigarette smoke, and BO wafting off the bootlegger.

As dusk fell into darkness, a battered blue Plymouth pulled to the curb in front of the house. A driver delivering two new girls; he shuffled up behind them, halting just inside the door. Removed his hat, twirled it in his hands. After showing the new girls upstairs to their rooms, Bessie returned and waited for the stranger to speak.

"How do, ma'am. Your mother around?"

"No, sir. She in jail. Can I help you?" Bessie asked.

"I'm Steve. I bring the girls from Philly. Have a place in New Kensington where they spend the night. In a couple of weeks, I'll pick them up and bring two new girls."

"Yes, I know the routine."

"Well, 's about time you paid me my cut."

"Your cut?" Bessie asked, her brows knitting.

"Running the girls. Gas ain't cheap. I've got bills. You gotta pony up with your fair share of expenses."

"Why don't you come out to the kitchen and give me the particulars." Bessie sighed.

Shortly after Steve's visit, the prostitution business quietly resumed. Bessie bought a black, leather-bound ledger called the preference book to note what customers liked and a receipt book to record the cash flow. She listed the customer's name, date, the amount paid, and sexual inclinations (1600 total patron entries). She kept the proceeds in a locked box anchored to a bottom drawer until she could deposit funds in the bank.

On bank day, after breakfast of biscuits and gravy, Bessie washed and powdered her face. She shimmied into her slip, her calico day dress falling to her ankles, stepped into sturdy black shoes, and her one extravagant purchase for herself: a fawn-colored, street-length mink coat. In her bedroom, she topped her outfit with a flannel floppy felt hat adorned with a single pheasant feather. Pulled her bag of money out of the closet.

She met Marion, who lived two houses down in the alley. A red felt flower flopped on her matching cloche as she hurried along, drawing her wool coat closed. "Mornin', cold today! My, don't you look fancy in your furs!"

"Thanks. Expect to wear it for the rest of my life!" Bessie laughed.

Sparse snowflakes danced in the air. High Street thronged with holiday shoppers. Windows were framed with red and green garlands. In the corner of one plate-glass window, a Kronenberg advertisement in *The Carlisle Evening Herald* was taped on the glass door. It suggested Christmas presents: "for the women, a pattern for a white lace collar with a list that included silk kimonos, fur coats or shirtwaist dress; for men, a housecoat or bathrobe; for boys, pajamas or suits, and for the little girls, a set of furs and Indian . . . suit," etc.[24]

Bessie strolled past the display to the Carlisle Electric & Gas Company office at 7 West High Street and paid cash to have 20 East Locust dwelling wired for electricity—a Christmas present to her family. At the square, she stopped as a Model T lumbered past. The Todd family's carriage wheeled the other way, the horses' harness bells jingling. At the intersection, she gestured for a church deacon and his wife to cross first. They stepped into the intersection with a nod of thanks.

When Miss Bessie and her sister walked into the (Commonwealth) bank on North Hanover Street, Jones's banker noticed their attire: black heels, print dresses, coats, gloves, and hats. Miss Bessie's floppy hat covered her ebony curls; the women had powdered their faces white, likely because C. J. Walker's cosmetics for African Americans had not yet gained national prominence.

Jones was toting a bag of cash, thousands of dollars, to deposit.

"Morning, Miss Jones," the Trust officer said as he stood and extended his hand. "Mrs. Middleton."

"How you doin', Mr. R.?" Bessie asked.

"Good mornin'," Marion responded, her eyes glancing at the tellers wearing green visors, standing at the long counter behind the bars.

"Fine as a fiddle. Winter's coming on. Looks like you have a warm coat there."

"Yessir. Don't much like cold weather." She huddled into her coat. "Don't have a choice 'bout the weather, so I bought a warm coat. Have a nice day, hear?" She stepped in line for the next teller to deposit her cash.

Mr. R nodded, returning to his desk. "She's a nice, gentle soul," he later told his wife.

Marion had to run another errand, so Bessie trekked down Hanover Street to Woolworth's alone. Overhead frosted tulip lights lit the long aisles; she paused at the rows of bright red and green glass ornaments. The sign exclaimed, "Decorate Your Christmas Trees!" Shelves filled with merchandise flanked the long walls. She selected hemmed handkerchiefs and leather wallets for her brothers; silk stockings for Marion and Vermont, ceramic mugs for the regular girls, and a new flannel nightgown for Cora for the cold nights in the jail.

Next to the mugs, three tiers of glassware glistened, winking at the lights. Strolling down another aisle, she picked up a 'church key' for opening bottles and cans, nearly colliding with one of her regular patrons, who tipped his hat in recognition and gestured for her to precede him.

Bessie smiled, nodded, and stepped up to the cashier to pay for her purchases.

"The Christmas ornaments are on sale," the salesclerk noted. She pointed to the sign, "One dollar a dozen!"

"Hmm. OK. I'll take a dozen red ones."

Trudging home with her gifts, she dropped them at the house and stepped back into the frigid air to go to the grocer for dinner fixings. With list in hand, she stopped to look in an appliance window at the cylindrical tub topped with rollers and a hand crank. "We could use a wringer-washer. But I'll get a telephone first."

CHAPTER 6

CASTING STONES

Tolling bells, resounding from a dozen church towers, called Carlislers to church on Sunday mornings. Bessie and her sisters donned their Sunday suits, pinned hats in place, pulled on gloves, and walked to the Black Presbyterian Church. Al and Willie were harder to corral, the first because he preferred bars; the second often traveled to Saratoga. Finding their seats, the women exchanged greetings with their neighbors and others. The choral director led the choir in the first hymn. As the congregation moved through the familiar program, singing hymns, listening to announcements, and offering prayers, the reverend finally stepped up to the podium.

"Today's we'll turn to John 8:1 to 11 for the Bible reading." In a clear, deep voice, he described Jesus coming down from the Mount of Olives, encountering the Pharisees, who caught a woman in the act of adultery. "Under Moses's law, they said, she would be stoned to death. 'What do you say, Master?' They waited for an answer as Jesus was busy writing in the dirt. When he finally straightened and addressed them, saying, 'He that is without sin, let him first cast a stone at her.'" One by one, the men dropped their rocks and walked away.

The reverend repeated the verse for emphasis. "Amens" punctuated his words. He paused. "Yes, that's our lesson today—not damnation for the sin of adultery but the balm of forgiveness! Not judgment but redemption! Let your conscience forgive sin in others just as your Father in Heaven forgives your sins." He warmed to his theme, pointing to them for emphasis. "Judge not, lest ye be judged!"

After the service, the church door opened, children scattered, darting around the adults, and chasing after one another. The reverend stood in the doorway, shaking hands and bidding, "Good day and God speed" to each. "And bless you, Mrs. Bessie Jones."

Bessie smiled. "And to you, preacher!" A weak winter sun warmed the air as the family wended its way to 20 East Locust Street past motorcars and horse carriages parked along the street. At intervals, stinking horse dung soured the air. Men followed with shovels and wheelbarrows to scoop up the steaming piles.

"What's for Sunday dinner?" Vermont asked. "Maybe we'll come over."

"Meatloaf today. It's in the icebox. Just have to put it in the oven. Marion, what about you making a pie?" Bessie asked.

"How about pumpkin again? I strained the last of it yesterday and put it in the icebox."

"An' I'll bring ice cream!" Vermont offered.

"And how about that? Dinner already half done," Bessie said. "Give us an hour or so to change outta our Sunday best." She reached for her key to unlock the front door.

Later, Bessie answered the rapping at the front door, admitting two new girls attired in boots, worn wool coats over fringed flapper dresses, cloche hats, and gloved hands clutching roomy, round hat boxes.

"You're late. Come in." Bessie peered around them, searching for their driver, then backed into the room, admitting them. "But welcome to Bessie's. My, those are snazzy dresses."

"They're all the rage! Aren't they marvelous?" Mary jiggled enough to make the fringe wiggle. "The motorcar broke down or stalled, so the driver had to find a mechanic. We were stuck and spent the night at his place in New Kensington. I'm Mary," said the tall, light-skinned Black woman. She had arched eyebrows, wide dark eyes, in a comely oval face. Her lips were painted crimson; her nails matched the lipstick.

"It's the Roaring Twenties, after all!" claimed the second girl. "And I'm Gloria." She had a flawless, fair complexion with pink cheeks and a thin smile, a joint cupped in her right hand.

Bessie peered out in the alley again for the Tin Lizzie. No parked vehicles stood at the curb.

"How old are you?" Bessie asked the second girl as she ushered them into the house.

"Twenty-one." Gloria smiled. "Don't worry; I'm experienced!" She took a drag. Held, then released it.

"There's an ashtray." Bessie pointed to a glass amber square on the end table next to the lamp. Gloria tapped out the burning end but retained the butt.

"Where shall we stash our stuff?" Mary stepped to the bottom of the stairs.

"Come along; I'll show you." Bessie filed ahead, leading the girls to the sparse upstairs bedrooms. "You'll bring the johns here. Everything you need you'll find in the nightstands, including rubbers." She pointed to the first and second bedrooms. "But you'll sleep upstairs."

"In the attic?" asked Gloria, her brows furrowed.

They climbed the last flight of stairs. Bessie opened the door. "Yes. You got twin beds with warm army blankets and two chests o' drawers with clean lingerie in sizes ten and twelve. There's a washbasin, soap, and stand, but you'll have to haul up your water from downstairs. Might want t'heat the teakettle 'cause we some-times run out of hot water.

"I fix breakfast at eight or so. We open for business from 10 A.M. to 1 A.M. Grab lunch on your own. If you're busy, I'll make sandwiches. Help yourself to what's in the pantry or icebox. We try to keep peanut butter and homemade jam on hand. Some-times we have leftover soup and keep apples and oranges, when we can get them, in the crisper. We take a supper break between ten and eleven in th'evening, earlier if it's a slow night.

"I have a few rules, like getting annual physicals and looking for VD symptoms for yourselves and your customers, but we can go over them after you settle in," she added. "You want to stay healthy."

"Ah, you in charge?" Mary turned to face the new Madam.

"I am. Mama's retired but still cooks for us, but she's not here now. 'Cause this your first night, we're serving supper early. Come on down when you're ready. You can help yourselves to water or milk from the icebox. I'll show you the percolator and coffee and tea canisters in case you're early risers. And you have a few chores—like doing the dishes, making your beds, and changing sheets daily."

"What if johns come now?"

"We're closed on Sundays," Bessie answered. She lumbered back downstairs to start dinner.

Marion and Vermont joined them for meatloaf, mashed potatoes, collard greens, and pumpkin pie. Mary tucked into the meal while Gloria picked at hers.

For the next five months, business at East Locust Street ran smoothly, quietly, and without incident.

After Cora Andrews returned to the brothel on May 14, 1923, Detective John Bush raided the house and arrested her, assuming she still ran the cat house. This time Andrews hired Herman Berg to represent her. Again, she pled guilty and paid her fine and court costs.[25] The law returned in June and July with arrest warrants. It appears the courts were intent on shutting her down.

On July 12, 1926, a local murder garnered much press attention, which took the spotlight off Bessie's business. An enraged and rejected suitor, Norman Morrison, marched up to his lover's front porch at 114 East Louther Street, where Frances Stuart (Bowermaster) lived with her three daughters and shot her three times, then turned the gun on himself. She died; he lived, but the self-inflicted bullet blinded him. Mildred, 17; Helen, 11; and Georgia, 3; lost their mother.[26]

Before her violent death, Bowermaster filed for divorce from her abusive husband; she hired Hyman Goldstein as her lawyer. He would also represent Bessie Jane Jones for the next thirty-five years, defending her from the onslaught of the moral majority who condemned her and her place of business while White businessmen, lawyers, and legislators continued to flock to her door. The law, district attorney, and judge brought charges against Madam Jones repeatedly. Yet those in power failed to shut her place down.

CHAPTER 7

BREAKING THE BANKS

On "Black Tuesday," October 29, 1929, the stock market crashed, the effects resonating around the world. Some investors lost all—changing from wealthy financiers to paupers overnight. Radio stations blasted news of men jumping from Wall Street windows. A decade of building factories, establishing and expanding businesses (often from loans) put most of the wealth in the hands of a few. At the same time, the average workers plodded along, scarcely keeping food on the table. With no money circulating, production and progress halted. Businesses closed, banks failed, and rising unemployment created hardship across the nation. Breadlines formed; landlords evicted renters, and mounting debt forced many into bankruptcy. Ousted from their homes, thousands squatted in cardboard boxes topped with sheet metal roofs. In cities, squatters scavenged scraps from the garbage.[27]

Carlisle also suffered through The Great Depression, which slammed the Black community hard. In a time of privation, the citizens learned to do without coffee, butter, flour, meat, eggs, and other staples. Unless one lived on a farm or tilled a garden, meat and fresh vegetables became scarce. Kids wore threadbare, ragged clothes insufficient to keep them warm in winter. They ran barefoot through the streets. They chased coal trucks to grab the chunks that tumbled to the street. Through those lean years, fortunate children fell on their Christmas stockings, thrilled to find an orange, a piece of hard candy, or hand-knitted mittens; the ones in dire straits received nothing. Many resorted to begging. Thousands of others lost parents to disease or, a dozen years later, the war.

Children in the big cities fared worse; they had to compete with the rats for food. Homeless, they sought shelter under eaves or condemned buildings—gangs formed for protection. Naïve but well-intentioned adults shipped orphans from New York City on trains as indentured servants to farmers in the Midwest and West who needed workers.[28] Some of the orphans fared well enough, working long hours for room and board; others resented their harsh treatment, rebelled and ran away. The abused children were reassigned. In other cases, teens left school to work to earn enough to eat and keep the family intact. In most towns and cities, many went to bed hungry.

As stores shut their doors in Carlisle, Sears and Roebuck supplied women with mail-order catalogs to pour over the new wares and later use them as toilet tissue when the sales book expired. Years later, a special edition called *The Wish Book* featuring toys appeared in November. Woolworth and local shops provided necessities. People learned to substitute, to make their soap or do without.

At the helm of the nation, FDR reassured Americans in his Fireside Chats "that the only thing we have to fear is . . . fear itself." His radio messages continued for over a decade—a stalwart voice of reason and security during the long, weary years when people suffered through the Depression and war years. In his first one hundred days, FDR proposed the Social Security Act, among many others. In his second hundred days, he continued pushing social reform through Congress that encouraged unions and aided farmers. Later he won an unprecedented third term as president—a symbol of hope and decisive leadership in those war-weary years.

To break the grip of the Depression, FDR's New Deal programs like the Civilian Conservation Corps (CCC) put unemployed men back to work. For example, in Carlisle, the Army Corps of Engineers oversaw building the stone walls that reinforced Letort Creek. Others paved the roads or erected buildings in the federal and state parks, including the secret POW Interrogation Camp beyond Pine Grove in Michaux Forest that incarcerated German and Japanese POWs. The Public Works Association (PWA) forced "industries to set minimum wages and fair prices, set the workweek hours, and gave workers the right to collective bargaining. The Tennessee Valley Authority built hydroelectric dams and led conservation measures."[29]

Luckily, Madam Jones had funds to cover expenses and dole out help to the Black community. She shared dinners with neighbors. When hungry children passed by, she handed them coins and fruit. Her thrift extended to donations to church groups, scouts, camps, and other charities, including those her mother had contributed to.

Cora Andrews helped shave expenses like knitting, patching, and sewing garments; they all made sacrifices.

"Look, Bess, I can cut the silk lining out of my everyday coat to make nighties for the girls. Maybe get two, but they're gonna be short." A week later, she returned to Bessie's Place with her sleeveless creations trimmed with eyelet lace. "While I'm here, I'll put the pot on and make some soup."

"Double the batch. People coming to the backdoor near every night." Bessie inspected the nighties. "Thank you, mama. They're mighty cute."

And though business slowed, Bessie's Place stayed open. The lawyers, police, and judges, though leaner, still knocked at the door, greeted Mary, Gay, Gloria, or another prostitute on the premises. They enjoyed their leisure; laid down their dollars for sex and liquor. The soldiers on leave or assigned to the Post came too, dressed as civilians. The men followed the girls upstairs, turned on by those nighties that barely covered the girls' bare buttocks.

"You look like a baby doll," one said. The men came back down the stairs smiling. Those waiting for a turn danced with the girls to the ragtime music broadcast over the radio or on the Victrola. Afterward, they sat down, Jack Daniels or beer in hand, and shared a late meal of soup and bread. Sometimes a fruit cobbler, pie, or bread pudding appeared for dessert.

"Com'on," Marion said as she met her sister at the foot of the courthouse steps after one of her encounters with the cops. "Yer workin' too hard. Stress putting frowning lines on yer face. Let's go to the picture show." She put her arm through her sister's and pulled her down High Street.

"Can't now that Mama's aging." Bessie pulled away. "There's so much to do: training new girls, buying their fancies, trying t'make ends meet, and feeding the neighborhood! Patrolling the door. Keeping accounts and paying the bills. Still trying to put money by for emergencies. Gotta shop for groceries now."

"Where's brother Will?"

"He went to Saratoga."

"What's in Saratoga?" Marion asked.

"Horses," Bessie replied. "Gotta have a backup plan. He's got a knack for picking winners."

Mornings, the milk wagon still delivered, the chestnut mare with a white blaze down her forehead clip-clopped down the street at dawn. The milkman left milk bottles in a metal box on stoops or porches. Doctors made house calls. The postman made his rounds. Businesses with meager wares to sell opened their doors.

Bessie still walked along Carlisle streets to pay her bills. She opened her change purse to pay the little tow-headed paperboy who trudged along in rain or snow, a burlap bag of newspapers slung across his shoulder. Opening *The Sentinel's* front page, a banner exclaimed: "Babes Found in the Woods!":

"The bodies of Norma Sedgwick, 12; Dewilla Noakes, 10; and Cordelia Noakes, 8; were discovered side by side under a blanket [near] Pine Grove Furnace on November 24, 1934. The girl's father, Elmo Noakes, suffocated them, likely because he couldn't afford their care. Later he shot and killed his eighteen-year-old niece, Winifred Pierce, and turned the twenty-two on himself. Carlisle held a public viewing to identify the girls who were from California. The American Legion paid for their funerals, and Boy Scouts served as pallbearers."[30]

The media published the tragic events nationwide. This poignant story conveys the dire straits and desperate measures that ordinary people endured in the hungry years leading up to World War II.

All was quiet on Carlisle's East End for nearly a decade while Madam Jones plied her trade, switching out prostitutes every two or three weeks. Tending to her chores, her routine set. She fixed breakfast; Cora cooked supper; the girls helped themselves to a quick lunch between assignations. Her liquor arrived at intervals during the night. Clients lined up, counting their money.

During that time, Grover Hunt, a Dickinson College maintenance employee, and a student, Linwood Gage, cut crystals in the basement of Conway Hall while Professor W.A. Paulen and three other students also experimented with quartz crystals. As a result, Standard Peizo opened for business in Carlisle in 1936. These crystals, or peizoelectricity, "detect[ed] and isolat[ed] message-carrying signals."[31] P.R. Hoffman's did the grinding and received a patent for the lap machine they developed.[32] The United States Army decided to use these "little wafers" in radios. The company, one of the few private businesses with a government contract, was soon working around the clock making crystals for radios. At the Corner of Cedar and West Louther Streets, the workers had a clear view of Bessie's place. They watched and gossiped about the jazz going on in and behind the brothel.

Jones's sister, Vermont, died in 1937. No details accompany her death notice, save that she deeded the 20 East Locust Street domicile back to her mother, her siblings, and her niece, Ruth Ahl, and nephew, Frank Ahl.[33]

Bessie Jones was first arrested as Madam, arraigned, and appeared in court on September 18, 1939, for "running a bawdy house." Her lawyer, Hyman Goldstein, entered her guilty plea. Because it was her first offense as the owner, the judge fined and charged her court costs. She huffed a sigh of relief. "Come have one on the house," she said to Goldstein.

He smiled but declined.

With the New Year came bone-soaking cold, snow, and the raw wind whipped coats and slapped bare faces. Citizens leaned into the gusts, hands clamped on hats and fedoras. They abandoned their motorcars—no gas available—and cycled or walked. Gas stations closed; new motorcars rusted on the lots since few could afford to buy them.

January 1940

"Com'on, I'm asking again. Let's go to the picture show to see *Gone with the Wind.* You'll be sorry to miss this. Everbody's talkin' about it," Marion said as they descended the courthouse steps.

"You don't have to ask me twice," Bessie said. "Nothin' like that hot buttered popcorn. Wonder if they still sell that for a quarter."

"What'd you think about the movie?" Leaving the theater, Marion buttoned her coat against the bitter chill. "Tara's a beautiful plantation."

"Yes, maintained by slaves! Imagine, Whites owned Blacks! Bought and sold them like cattle. I read runaways were beaten, whipped—or worse. Children sold away from their parents. Heard plantation owners raped the slave women 'n sold off their children! Be glad you live here.

"I think Hattie Daniels overdid it a bit screaming 'Miss Scarlet!'" Bessie waved her hands, imitating Daniels on the landing in the movie. "Seemed like White folks nostalgic for life before the Civil War." Bessie leaned on her cane.

"But you have to admit, 'Scarlet, I don't give a damn,'" Marion insisted, "was a great last line for Rhett Butler."

"Yeah, that gal's beautiful but selfish. Determined, though— gotta hand her that. And resourceful—that velvet drapery dress!"

"Ooo. That was beautiful!"

In 1940, Richard Wright published *Native Son,* an angry depiction of the Negro Bigger Thomas growing up in a White world: "he learned to be passive in the face of White aggression, that in fact, the best protection in a White world was invisibility."[34] Thomas took out his rage by bullying his buddies, but Madam Jones adopted a more positive attitude while striding that thin line between acceptance and rejection. She smiled and greeted passersby on the streets, despite the whispers behind her back and the gossip that found its way to her door.

"I'm from Carlisle, born and raised," she mumbled as the cane tapped a tattoo on the sidewalks, her floppy hats varied as to the season, and her doors remained open for business. "And here I'll stay."

Again, on January 20 and May 9, 1941, Liquor Control Board agents arrested Jones for "selling liquor without a license."[35] During sentencing, the Madam's stoic face wore a mask of indifference or defiance. On the way out, the courthouse steps quaked with munitions thundering from Fort Indian Town Gap.

CHAPTER 8

THE NATION DECLARES WAR

On December 8, 1941, President Franklin Delano Roosevelt declared war on Japan, the day after that island nation attacked and destroyed half the Naval fleet at Pearl Harbor. The United States had officially entered World War II. After issuing the first draft and calling up the National Guard, FDR sent Americans to the European and Asian theatres to battle fascism and imperialism.

At home, the Ford Company rolled out Sherman tanks and Liberty engines, Boeing welded and assembled airplanes, and productions of machine guns and munitions ramped up. "Uncle Sam" and "Rosie the Riveter" posters plastered windows. Pennsylvania displayed a poster of a threatening Uncle Sam, with the words, "Jap, you're next." Men and women enlisted in the Armed services, anxious to serve on the front lines. Pennsylvania sent 667,000 men and 12,913 women into the Army, Navy, Marines, and Coast Guard; only New York sent more soldiers into war.[36]

Nationwide, thousands of women joined the WACS and WAVES. The federal government and the armed services recruited women from colleges to go to Washington to train as code breakers, decoding enemy missives and gaining intelligence of German, Italian, and Japanese diplomatic dispatches. Sworn to silence and secrecy, the codebreakers worked twenty-four-seven deciphering enigmatic, complicated alphabetic and numeric codes and relaying crucial information for the allies to intercept enemy submarine routes, bombing raid timetables, troop movements, and transport missions.[37]

"The home front rarely gets equal credit, but World War II required such a massive build-up on factory and assembly lines or in shipbuilding yards, in government offices and top-secret laboratories, on farms and ranches, the men and women who stayed behind were fully immersed in the war effort."[38]

In *The Greatest Generation,* Tom Brokaw recorded stirring anecdotes about the stalwart Americans who left their routines and faced the death machine called the Third Reich in Europe and the vicious Japanese troops in the Pacific.

The Red Cross mobilized nurses and first-aid materials with the volunteers rolling gauze for bandages and making blackout curtains and care packages. Women and African Americans swelled the workforce. Large homes or manors in the allied countries became hospitals.

So many outstanding authors like Winston Churchill, Dwight D. Eisenhower, David McCullough, Doris K. Goodwin, and others have dedicated much time, energy, and effort in chronicling the World War II years from 1941 to 1945; their books recount the allied soldiers' sacrifices, the bloody battles, the hard-won victories, and the horrific losses. The heroes who returned lived with the hell they had faced. From the coders and those in all the Armed Services—the men and women who toiled four agonizing years and the ones who guarded the hearth—deserve *The Greatest Generation* appellation.

Hollywood produced newsreels supporting allied victories; producers cranked out patriotic war films showing bombing raids and tank maneuvers. Celebrities like Bob Hope, Francis Langford, and Danny Kaye joked, sang, and danced for the troops at American bases. When pin-up models like the most popular Bette Grable joined the entertainers, the uniformed crowds whistled and cheered. Celebrities too numerous to list joined the armed forces as well, enlisting to serve their country.

On March 4, 1945, Cora Andrews died. The Presbyterian Church held the services; the Schulenberger Funeral Home handled burial details. Except for her four surviving grown children, few people attended. Afterward, Carlisle's Madam of "Cora's Place" was interred in the old Union Cemetery.[39]

Here in Carlisle, people contributed to the war effort. Conserved. Planted victory gardens. Canned the produce. Endured four years of ration cards. Made sacrifices. Learned to scrimp and do without. People had to cut cardboard soles to tuck in shoes worn to the pavement. Used newspapers to line their coats and insulate their homes. Postponed their goals and dreams. Women replaced the fighting men in the workforce; the jobs put money in the family purse again. However, most commodities were unavailable for the average consumer and impossible for the Black community to obtain:

The War Production Board reported on May 10, 1945 news article that: companies making large appliances, passenger cars, and other commodities would take three years to meet the civilian demand: "Consumer radios will be available within the year, passenger cars, six-nine months. In twelve months, civilian items will be back on shelves."[40] By the fall, some staples reappeared on grocer's shelves. Technology fueled more jobs in print and broadcast journalism, the auto industry, for the war machine, and in medicine.

Allied soldiers were mopping up in Europe, a crumbling wasteland. The German army had confiscated food, supplies, and shelter for their soldiers. Commandeered radios, raw materials, and equipment for their war machines. Stole artwork and stored it in caves. Destroyed property and killed thousands of civilians—forced Jews, gypsies, and resistance members into concentration camps. Sadistic SS officers, armed with German Shepherds, whips, and rifles, controlled the people, trains, and roads. Worked the able-bodied to death. Paid informants to snitch on neighbors. War correspondents radioed the gut-churning news across the airwaves.

As the war dragged on, the United States, with the UK and Canada, participants were sworn to secrecy as they labored on a nuclear device that would cause a chain reaction—the atomic bomb. The 1945 test resulted in success. Later a group at Los Alamos worked furtively and frantically on developing a nuclear weapon—competing with German scientists for the ultimate weapon. Dr. Robert Oppenheimer and Major General Leslie Grove led the research team on the Manhattan Project to develop a more powerful hydrogen bomb.[41]

Fighting continued in the Pacific. The Pentagon had considered a ground assault on mainland Japan. More boots on the ground meant more American causalities, further conflict, and more complex multilateral treaties. Therefore, on August 6, 1945, President Truman targeted Hiroshima for the first atomic bomb because Japan had refused to surrender unconditionally. Still, Emperor Hirohito refused to surrender. Truman ordered a second hit on Nagasaki. Then Japan surrendered unconditionally.

Edward R. Murrow and others broadcast from Great Britain: "The Japs have surrendered!"

CHAPTER 9

HONEY FOR BISCUITS

On a slow night, Bessie and the girls tuned into President Roosevelt's Fireside Chat, advising Americans as the war dragged on that our soldiers and citizens were united against tyranny. That the Allies were battling for their homeland. Newscasters reported the Allies' hard-won victories and demoralizing defeats. Finally, the Madam turned the dial off. "Maybe the worst is over. Let's go to bed. We're all tired, but we have to do our part, too." The girls retreated to the attic room, removed their makeup with cold cream, and undressed. Bessie brought up the steaming teakettle to warm their wash pans.

"Thank you, ma'am," they said in unison.

"Breakfast at eight," Madam said, descending the stairs into her bedroom to remove her makeup, wash up and brush her teeth. She rolled off her stockings, tucked them into her shoes, and donned her a nightgown. Turned down the covers and crawled into bed.

Upstairs in the attic, the girls readied for bed. "What's so funny all of a sudden?" Gloria asked Mary, slipping out of her negligee, and tossing it in the hand-wash basket. She tugged a flannel nightgown over her head. A button caught in her hair; she eased them apart.

"That last customer, the poor man, said his wife wouldn't have sex with him until after the baby is born." Mary soaped up her washcloth and passed it across her face, working her way down her body. "He has four more months to wait. Can you imagine?"

"Would banging hurt the baby?" the younger woman asked, her face blanched like flour, Ivory bubbles flecking her chin. She paused in her ablutions to peer at her roommate.

Mary shrugged. "I don't know." She stepped into a flannel nightgown. "Think it's OK to a certain point."

"I've heard every excuse in the book—like most wives won't do half and half. Well, I don't enjoy sucking cocks either. But we ain't gotta choice, and I get that we're trash. No little girl wants to be a prostitute when she grows up! My parents died in the war 'n I had nowhere to go, no money for food or rent.

"But get this one—'I have a headache.' Do they think oral sex is nasty?" Gloria slipped into her long johns and pulled on knitted wool socks. "Ah, warmth!"

"I agree—nothin' worse than a dirty dick. There are worse things, like getting our asses beat by a pimp. Using make-up to cover our bruises. Yanking us by the hair. Fear of the clap or other VD's. That's why we stay away from the streets. I imagine the wives have reasons. Could be some are squeamish about sex. Or afraid," Mary observed.

"Afraid? Why?" Gloria's eyebrows quirked.

"My, you are young. Because their mothers told them sex is dirty or disgusting—or worse, told their daughters nothing at all. Or their men like it rough; some don't take no for an answer, so intercourse hurts because their wives aren't ready. I'll bet many men don't care about foreplay. Or maybe women haven't ever come. Maybe too many kids already. And pregnant single women are forced into shotgun weddings or—go to that Harrisburg doctor for an abortion.[42] Or give the baby up. Many die from self-inflicted abortions."

"Then some are ignorant or inexperienced about sex? But blame us?"

"That's part of it, but they may not know about rubbers. Or their men don't like them. Remember, Catholics forbid contraception. Despite all the churches, people darting dirty looks at us and gossiping behind our backs say a lot about the town. Well, and the fact that's prostitution's illegal here. Still, for many women, sex is a chore."

"And calling us dirty whores. I get the single gents wanting fresh trim, but if wives took care of their men at home, they wouldn't come here." Gloria rolled down the blanket and slipped between the sheets, pulling the wool blanket up to her neck. "I hate it when people spit at us."

"Get used to it. We are whores—a gal's gotta eat." Mary turned off the bare overhead bulb.

"Goodnight."

"It's one A.M."

"Get some sleep, smartass."

Weeks later, while Rosemary and Marion were entertaining their johns, Bessie pulled the hambone from the fridge, bits of meat clinging to the bone. She drained the water from the navy beans that had soaked all night. "Let's see if this works."

In the yard, she dug up wild garlic, chopped the strands and dropped the bone in the soup pot, added fresh water and the softened beans. She lit the stove under it. She rummaged through the stove drawer until she located the lid and cocked it so the pot wouldn't boil over. Soup and bread for supper. Then she sat, the sentinel at the front door until midnight or until the last john straggled out.

The next morning, Jones heard the girls in the basement feeding their sheets through the wringer on top of the washing machine. A rooster cock-a-doodle-doed! The milkman thunked the glass bottles into the metal bin on the front porch. Six am. The sun spilled over the horizon, radiating golden light a ribbon at a time.

"Mama, I miss you." Bessie trudged into the kitchen, Heated the oven. "Add dry ingredients. Cut the butter into the flour 'til they look like peas," she repeated Cora's instructions. Poured in the buttermilk, kneaded, and formed a circle of dough. Floured the counter, rolled out the dough, and cut biscuit rounds. Fitted them into an iron skillet. "Into the oven you go." While the biscuits baked, she opened the fridge and pulled out three eggs, whisking them to a mellow yellow. Poured them into a hot skillet and stirred.

Still wearing nightgowns, Gay and Rosemary carried the basket up the stairs and outside to hang the sheets on the line and prop them up with a six-foot notched pole. "Windy, so they'll dry by the time we open," one remarked.

The door banged open. "Mornin' y'all!" Marion greeted them with a wide smile. "Did you hear the news? Japan surrendered! No more rationing! No more makin' do with next to nothing. And we're the lucky ones! Those poor Brits and Europeans bombed to bits. Can you imagine having to pick through the rubble to find pieces of your past, like your wedding photo? Nothing to wear, nowhere to go. No shoes to wear. Gotta feel sorry for all those countries." She shook herself, changed the subject. "Look! I brought honey for the biscuits!" She held up the jar of amber.

"Real honey?" Rosemary cried, her stomach rumbling. "Come on in."

"Want an egg?" Bessie asked her.

"Honest to God honey! No, thanks, jus' a biscuit an' honey. The war is over. Finally. Four long years! Lord be praised! Our men be coming home. Oh, sorry, Bessie—not your man, Willie.

Did you ever hear from him after the first war? But just think about buying shoes again. Or drinking real coffee instead of that awful chicory stuff."

Bessie's face froze. "I don't want to talk about it."

"Some soldiers won't be coming back," Gay said. "Sad to think of how many we lost: thousands of dads, brothers, husbands, and fiancés gone. Or mothers, sisters, wives, or fiancées. Buried in graves across the ocean. Never again to see a sunny morning like this one."

"The Allies halted Hitler's murdering rampage and liberated the concentration camps," Gay stated. "I'm glad he's gone. And those Jap butchers! Did you hear about their brutality in their POW camps? Giving prisoners infested gruel and scraps while the Japanese kept the Red Cross boxes for themselves. That's mighty low. Wasn't there a law against that?"

"Criminals don't follow the law. We're lucky; we have more than most. We still got a roof over our heads, food in our bellies, and clothes on our backs. Okay, girls, time's a-wasting. Take your coffee upstairs. Get ready for your johns. Marion, since you're here, heat the kettle for the girls. I've got to get dressed, laundry to do. I need to go to Wardecker's for sexy new lingerie." She sopped up the rest of her yolk with a piece of warm biscuit and then dribbled honey onto the second half. "Oh my, that's so good. Where'd you get it?"

"You sound like Mama." Marion filled the teakettle and placed it in on a burner next to the percolator. "A soldier brought it up from Gettysburg. Just stopped by the side of the road when he saw the hives at one of the orchards, and the farmer gave it to him. Then he bought another for us. Wasn't that nice?"

World War II officially ended on September 2, 1945. New York City held a ticker-tape parade with the iconic kiss between a sailor and a nurse immortalized on the front page of newspapers and *Life* magazine. Cities held parades, welcomed their husbands, brothers, fathers, sons, and uncles home. Opened their arms to mothers, daughters, sisters, and wives.

Of the 1.25 million Americans who served, 409,000 never returned, including all Armed services members, resistance fighters, POWs, and code breakers.[43] Families grieved in their own ways; others adjusted to those who returned too damaged to function, but with the G.I. Bill, returning soldiers could buy a house and start families or go to college.

The town returned to building, expanding, and welcoming more businesses like Sheaffer Brothers Sporting Goods; Pennsylvania Power and Light bought Cumberland Valley Electric, and M&Z Carpet relocated to Carlisle. The crystal industry splintered and changed hands. Masland & Sons flourished; in his retirement letter, Frank Masland stated his "company became an international carpet-making industry for Henry Ford and other auto manufacturers."[44] Miller's Realty, Cochran and Allen, Carlisle Cement, Billets Electric, and others forged ahead into a more promising decade, buoyed by a solid, reliable workforce.

CHAPTER 10

SOUP'S ON

Shambling out of bed, Jones slipped into her robe. The girls were stirring. They'd want breakfast. After splashing water on her face, she removed her hairnet and raked her stubborn curls up into a messy bun. Donning her black-framed glasses, she descended the stairs. "No time for biscuits today. Looks like a French toast kinda day." The iron skillet heated while she beat two eggs. Minutes later, she scattered three plates across the kitchen table. Spooned Maxwell House into the percolator's basket, filled the pot with water, and put it on the back burner. In a few minutes, it bubbled and popped, brewing.

"You're dressed in street clothes," Jones observed as the girls scraped the last of their syrupy toast off their plates.

"Just going for a walk. If Woolworth's is open, I need a new garter belt and nylons."

"I'm just tagging along."

"I have a rule that girls don't leave the house without me," Jones reminded them. "I'll buy your garments later; you girls can clean up the kitchen 'cause I want to put on a pot of soup. Clients'll be coming at ten. Are the bedsheets clean?"

After the grumbling girls left the dishes draining, Bessie sliced and browned onion, carrots, and celery into a tablespoon of bacon grease, stirred, and poured water in the pot. In went last night's chicken carcass to cook the meat off the bones.

Upstairs, silence met her. "Damn, those girls must've wandered off. Hard to get good help nowadays." She dressed in a black pleated skirt and print blouse, then trekked back downstairs to gently lift the chicken bones onto a tin pie plate to cool so she could debone them. She tested the steaming meat and snapped her hand back. "Ouch!"

At first, it sounded like squirrels scratching at the screen. A shadow crossed the window, but the shades were still drawn. The front door rattled. She picked up the phone receiver. She listened for a dial tone. A quivering index finger dialed the police number on the black rotary phone, the dial ticking back with every number.

"Help! I'm being robbed!" Bessie whispered. "Send a squad car to 20 East Locust Street quick!" The back door squeaked and quaked; the knob rattled. Out front, metal screeched and scraped the screen.

"I'll dispatch one right away. Are they in the house?"

"No, but one's cutting the screen at the front; the other's trying to bust in the door."

"Are you by yourself, ma'am?" the cop asked.

"Yes." The rattling and scraping crawled up her spine.

"Do you have money or valuable jewelry in the house?"

"What do you think, young man? I'm Bessie Jones! Yes. Please, I'm afraid. Hurry."

"Lock yourself in your closet or hide in the attic." He paused. "Can you stay on the line?"

"No, can't do both. I'll be damned if I hide in my own house!" She dropped the receiver into the cradle and scurried to the kitchen. Slipped her hands into hot pads.

Crash! The front door caved in. Heavy footsteps clomped across the floor. Two strangers wearing bandanas covering their noses and mouths and brandishing knives approached her. "Ve vant your whorin' money—ill-gotten gains!"

"Hand it over, or we'll tear this place apart," threatened the other, stepping closer.

Bessie picked up the pot of soup and heaved it over both.

"Ow! You bitch," The first one tried to brush off the burning liquid splattered across his face and shirt. The heavier one tugged his shirt away from his scalded body. Both tried hopping away from themselves.

Sirens whined; lights slashed across the window shades.

"It's about time!" Jones muttered to herself. "Y'all come here often enough uninvited." To the police, she exclaimed, "Thank God you got here in time! These strangers tried to rob me!"

"Are you hurt, ma'am?" asked the uniformed officer.

She shook her head. "No. Just shaken."

He pulled out a pocket notebook. "I need your statement."

Two other police arrested the two men, lugged them off to the Cumberland County Jail, and charged them with breaking and entering. The men were arraigned, charged with B&E, attempted robbery, and assault. They were bound over for a court trial; the case seemed open and shut.

Climbing up the concrete courthouse steps two weeks later, the building loomed over Bessie and Marion. The full weight of the justice system beyond those massive columns and wooden doors settled on Jones. The defense lawyers were ready to combat, state attorneys to prosecute, and judges to preside.

"You tired?" Marion paused too as members of the press jogged past them.

Old courthouse. (Courtesy of the Cumberland County Historical Society.)

"A little. This building makes me jumpy. But this time I'm not the defendant." They trod up the last steps arm in arm.

Bessie and Marion sat through the trial, which moved briskly. Bessie testified that two men had broken into her home, damaging windows and doors and demanded money.

"And what did you do?" asked District Attorney Harold Sheely.

"I threw a pot of hot soup on them."

The judge banged the gavel to stop the snickers and guffaws in the gallery. "Order in the courtroom!"

The D.A. then called Counter-intelligence Officer Duncock to the witness stand; he corroborated the facts.

"Were you able to identify the defendants?" the D.A. asked, pointing to the men beside the public defender.

"The men from Maryland are of European descent—German," said Duncock. Other witnesses followed, including the arresting police officer, substantiating Jones's account.

Sheely and the public defender summed up their cases. The judge advised the jury of its duty and options and sent them out. Returning from deliberation, avoiding Bessie's eyes, the jury filed into the courtroom and took their seats. The foreman, Earl Keim, stood to address the court, shaking his head. "We have a hung jury. Ten to two."[45]

The judge gaveled the court to attention. "I have no choice but to release these men because of time served."

The courtroom cleared; the press sprinted to print the story. Jones sat, stunned. Justice had failed her. She who usually admitted her guilt and paid her fines without complaint. Served her time in jail, suffering the demeaning treatment and epithets from the prison guards. The strangers who broke into her home, threatened her, and would have taken her money escaped justice. The outcome left blisters on her soul, but she refused to cry. Her face was a mask, a carapace sloughing off the wounding words. She let Marion help her up, pushed her arms into her coat, walked out and down the courthouse steps, the cane tapping. "That's not fair."

Marion agreed. "No, it's not. There's no justice for Black folks, never has been, never will be. We can't escape our history; our past is buried in our blood and our skin color. Well, an' there's the fact that we run a brothel . . ." Her sister's words were riven in the wind. Bessie nodded, too shocked to cry or speak that Lady Justice wasn't blind but biased.

Keim later confided to the press that two elderly ladies on the jury refused to convict and return a guilty verdict because the Maryland men didn't steal anything and because Jones "ran a house of ill repute."

Despite the disappointment, the 1950s saw seminal events build momentum for Blacks. In *Brown versus the Board of Education,* the Supreme Court ruled segregation unconstitutional; Rosa Parks refusing to give up her seat resulted in a year-long bus boycott in Montgomery, Alabama, proving the effectiveness of non-violent civil disobedience. During this time, President Eisenhower sent federal troops to enforce the integration law at Central High in Little Rock, Arkansas. An eloquent, committed, and inspired leader, Martin Luther King, emerged to lead the Civil Rights Era.

As a response to an op-ed letter signed by Birmingham religious leaders stating time was not right for such protests, King later argued persuasively in "Letter from Birmingham Jail" that time is neutral; it could be used constructively and destructively, and people had the right to disobey unjust laws.

The intense, sometimes violent struggle to gain equal rights gathered momentum in the 1960s with further boycotts, sit-ins at restaurants, and counter-protests. Police used clubs and water hoses to beat and break up the peaceful protesters. Slowly, the protestors gained traction. As a result, African Americans gained better access to elections and affirmative action; many garnered a college education and entry into white-collar jobs previously closed to them.

Time in Carlisle ticked off the days, weeks, and months with bustling business, new construction, and the Borough annexing more land. The Market House and Sentinel buildings were condemned and demolished. The newspaper relocated to its current location at 327 B Street. The Bellaire and David Swartz Intermediate schools were constructed, and new businesses like the Carlisle and MJ Malls opened. People focused on their routines while 20 East Locust Street continued its business.

CHAPTER 11

A STRANGER KNOCKS

"Thump, bang, thud!" The front door vibrated.

"What the hell! Who's banging on the door?" Bessie wondered.

The girls were upstairs entertaining men who'd waltzed in wearing pressed suits, triangles of handkerchiefs peeking from their left front pockets, and wide, striped ties. They strode in with an air of confidence that signaled success.

Jones opened the door to find a strange young woman wearing a pillbox hat, a short white jacket, and matching gloves over a navy print shirtwaist dress. She was pulling at her skirt while juggling a purse in one hand, cigarette in another. Her straight nut-brown hair fell to her chin, tips pitching forward. Freckles marched across her nose; her mouth set, her chin sharp and firm in an otherwise plain face. Her aqua eyes met the Madam's.

"Are you lost?" Jones looked up and down the street for her driver. An old snub-nosed tan Chrysler hunched at the curb. "Can I help you?"

"I hope so. Are you Mrs. Bessie Jones?" the young woman asked.

"Yes." Bessie stepped aside. "Won't you come in? How about a cup of coffee? I was just taking some cookies out of the oven." She turned, shuffled back to the kitchen to turn off the oven.

Poured coffee into a cup. 'How do you take it?" She sat an ashtray within her guest's reach.

"Just a little cream or milk. Thank you." She stubbed out her cigarette, laid her navy handbag on the kitchen table, and lowered herself onto a chair, taking in the worn wallpaper. Her eyes lighted on the record player, then the radio, and back to Jones. "I don't know where to start," she began.

"You could start with your name." Bessie pushed the cup and saucer across the table, placed a plate of tollhouse cookies in the middle, and sat opposite her guest.

"Oh, sorry. Yes. My name's Minnie. I'm a bit flustered. I've never done anything so bold as to knock on a stranger's door and ask for a job." Quivering fingers pulled out a hairpin, removed her hat, setting it on top of her purse.

Jones sipped from her mug. "Have a cookie." She took one still warm. "What kind of work are you looking for? I have a maid, and I do the marketing, cooking, and record keeping. My sister helps. So do the girls who live here while they work. Do you have any experience?" She bit down on the molten morsels and chewed.

Minnie's mouth opened and shut. She cleared her throat. "No, I've worked part-time here and there. Mainly secretarial work. My parents want me to get married, but . . ." A flush crawled up her neck to her cheeks. She sipped her coffee, then set the cup down.

Jones waited until Minnie composed herself.

Her guest finished her cookie. "Hmm, the cookie's delicious. Thank you." She cleared her throat. "I want to work for you." Her head nodded toward the stairs, where they could hear thumping and bumping. "You know. Upstairs."

"You want to be a prostitute?" Jones asked.

The girl nodded. "I want to try."

Jones wiped her mouth on a napkin. "Why?"

"I want to know what sex, ah, 'em—intercourse feels like. I want to earn my own money—not depend on my parents for everything. If I don't like it, what's the point of getting married? Face a lifetime of an obligation that I don't enjoy? Give up my freedom?"

"It's very irregular; I must say," Jones answered. "Whoring's not enjoyment; it's employment. It's work. Your job is to satisfy your customer, and, let me say, we get some strange requests." She described the various positions and acts the johns usually favored.

"Yes, I know. No, I mean, I don't *know,* but I understand what you're saying. I wouldn't stay here. My home's in Biglerville; I can commute. What if someone falls sick or has an accident and can't work? Someone told me you have two girls here at a time. Couldn't you use a third? Don't you sometimes have a rush? I've heard men line up outside the door."

Jones nodded. "They usually line up and wait."

"But why have them wait? If you had a third girl, they could just waltz right in, get down to business."

"Alright. Strip."

Minnie swallowed. "What?" Her hand flew to her chest.

"You heard me. Let's see what you've got under those clothes."

"Here? Now? What if someone comes in?"

"That's the idea. If you want to work, you need to get used to being naked."

"Girls sit around naked?" Blushing pinked her cheeks again.

"No, they wear lingerie. I don't think this is a job for you."

Minnie stood, tugged off her tailored jacket, and draped it across the chair's shoulders. She unbuttoned her shirtwaist, stepped out of it. Tossed it over her jacket. She hesitated. And then pulled her satin slip up and over her head. Dropped it on the dress. She reached back and unsnapped her bra.

The upstairs door opened; a man trooped down the stairs, shirtsleeves rolled up to his elbows, tie in hand, and suit coat slung over his shoulder. He froze at the foot of the stairs. Gay followed close behind but skirted around him and into the kitchen. The fridge door popped open. Liquid gurgled into a glass.

He stared as the young lady stepping out of her panties. Rotating toward the fit, handsome stranger, Minnie's face flushed radish red. Blue eyes slid up and down her firm breasts, thin waist, hesitated at the 'Y', roved lazily back up to her eyes. He stretched out his hand, curving two fingers in a come-hither gesture.

Minnie strode right up to him, took his hand; they turned and mounted the steps.

"New girl?" Gay asked, drinking milk, nibbling on a cookie.

"Apparently so." Jones stood. "What a world. And I thought I'd seen everything."

When Minnie trooped back down the stairs, all smiles after the stranger left, she handed Madam two twenties.

"But . . ." Jones began, taking a minute to process the amount, then shook her head. She handed Minnie a twenty back. "You were a virgin?"

Ginny nodded, a smile curving her lips. "Do I have that part-time job?"

"You do, starting now. Go upstairs to the attic bedroom and find yourself something sexy to wear."

CHAPTER 12

NABBED AGAIN

1959

The March winds blew knots of paper, candy wrappers, and stray leaves; it tunneled down Locust Street and whipped the tree skeletons. The branches clicked together like crickets. The sun peeked over the horizon, heralding another bright but chilly day. Madam Jones sipped hot coffee while putting scrambled eggs and toast on the table, smiling that business was humming along despite the weather.

Soon Joanne Ellis and Rosemary Jones tripped down the stairs, exchanging 'good morning' and chatting about spring.

"We could pot a tomato plant, keep it on the patio. We'd have fresh, off the vine, ripe red slices for our sandwiches," Joanne said.

"But will we be here when they're ripe? Or will everybody else eat them?" Rosemary joined Bessie Jones at the kitchen table and poured coffee for them both. Joanne added a spot of cream to hers. "Morning, Miss Bessie."

"Mornin' girls. How'd you sleep?" she asked, sitting down to her plate. The toast popped from the new toaster.

Joanne grabbed both slices, buttered them, handing one to Rosemary. Miss Bessie was already munching on her toast, lavished generously with butter. *The Sentinel* sat on the table beside her plate.

"Well," Joanne said. "The wind made a terrible racket, but other than that, we slept okay."

"You can melt candle wax for earplugs. Take care to let the wax cool but mold it to your ears when it's warm." Jones offered. "Or use cotton balls."

Joanne read the headline above the fold: "'Rockefeller Backs Fallout Shelters!' She savored a forkful of fluffy egg. "What's a fallout shelter?"

Rosemary answered, "It's politics. Rich guy wants to waste millions on underground bunkers in case an enemy drops a bomb on us."

"Oh, shit! Can that happen here?" Ellis peered at the article upside down. "It's about the cold war, isn't it?" She read the headline 'Fidel Castro Becomes Dictator of Cuba'."

"My paperboy says they practice 'duck and cover' drills at school under their desks. Scaring the poor kids like that." Jones swathed jam on her last triangle of toast and chewed.

Rosemary scoffed. "Like that'd help. Which cities?"

"You know, all the big cities like New York and Los Angeles." Joanne guessed. "But not Carlisle?" she wondered.

"Don't know, but don't worry; we have a basement. We can seal windows with plastic. Plenty of canned goods down there too. We could probably last a year. No use worrying 'bout what we can't fix." The Madam gathered her plate and rinsed it off, set it in the sink. "Whose turn to do dishes?"

"We usually do them together," Joanne said. "But I have the sniffles." She pulled a tissue out of her pocket and swiped her runny nose.

"We don't want nobody sick. Make yourself some ginger tea with honey. That'll help. Your throat sore?"

Ellis shook her head no; she knew Madam would send her to the doctor. "Just a cold. Do you, we, have rubbers? And Vicks?"

"Did you check your nightstand?" Jones asked her youngest girl. "If not, put it on the list. Oh, add vinegar and Kleenex too. Did you change the sheets? I have to run some errands, and Beatrice will be here in half an hour. We'll be wiping everything down with Lysol solution."

Joanne wrinkled her nose. "That stuff smells medicinal."

"Well, it kills germs. With so many people coming in and out, we got to keep the place sanitary."

Rosemary sprinkled some Breeze into the dishpan; a dishcloth fell out and plopped into the water. "Look, the free dishcloth! My little brother called them 'the free insides!' like we were gettin' something for nothing. I'll wash, you dry."

Jones mounted the stairs shaking her head. "Talking about tomatoes already. Too early to plant, and I can buy the best ones at farmer's market come May." In the bathroom, she removed her robe, splashed water on her face, and soaped the necessities. Dried off. Brushed her teeth; she felt one wobble. "Mental note, call the dentist."

She twisted her hair up—not much she could do with a mop of course, unruly curls. Opening her rouge cream, she dabbed both cheeks with color. Padded to her bedroom to get dressed. Tugged on nylons. Chose a pink blouse and grey wrap skirt. Grey loafers. Reached into her closet for a matching floppy hat. Donned her fur coat. Grabbed her cane and pocketbook.

Beatrice Ahl arrived. Bessie could hear the conversation between her and Rosemary and Joanne. The girls "Ooed and Ahhed" over something she brought. Then they clambered up the steps to the bedrooms, devouring the sweet rolls in three bites. Jones sniffed the air as the scent of cinnamon wafted up, surrounding her as she descended the stairs.

Back downstairs, the maid had already dragged the vacuum cleaner out of the hall closet. Her bucket of cleaning supplies stood ready. "Morning, Miz Bessie. Marion sent the cinnamon rolls."

Jones nodded. "I'll be back before lunch. If I'm not back by ten, will you let our patrons in if you recognize them?"

"Yes'm." Beatrice's head bobbed up and down as she plugged in the Kenmore.

"You need anything?"

"We're getting low on Clorox and Borax. Or I can pick them up when I'm done here. Your oven light's out too. I put the rolls in there on warm if you want one," Ahl stated.

"Thanks. Maybe later." She fought the door as the wind tugged it, and then pushed her weight against it until it latched. The wind whipped at her coat, but she held it firm. Once at Woolworth's, she hooked her cane on a basket and roamed the aisles, selecting the items on her list. She met Mrs. Shughart at the checkout counter.

"Mornin' Mrs. Shughart."

"Good day to you, too, Miss Bessie. Isn't this wind awful? That howling kept me awake last night."

"Well, ma'am, it is March. How's the judge?"

"Guess he's sitting on his bench about now. Did you see *The Sentinel* headlines?"

"About the fallout shelters? Yes, um. But don't think they'll come too much. We all have basements."

"Well, that's true enough. Still, it's worrisome. A dictator controlling Cuba might escalate the Cold War. Well, no use worrying about danger that we can't alter. I imagine the president will take care of it." Abruptly, she changed the topic. "Did you try that turkey casserole recipe I gave you a few weeks ago?"

"I did—last week, but I used chicken. It's easy and tasty—just dump the ingredients in a baking dish, pour the soup overall, sprinkle cheese on the top, and stick it in the oven. Thank you.

Woolworth's. (Courtesy of Cumberland County Historical Society.)

Well, I have to stop at A&P yet and get back to the house. We open in a half-hour."

"You have a good day, hear?" The judge's wife turned to the display rack at the checkout counter for a copy of *Ladies' Home Journal.*

"You too, Mary Ann." Bessie smiled. At A&P, she laid lettuce, apples, oranges, a bag of potatoes, onions, and chicken on the counter, checked out, paid cash, and walked home. The delivery boy pulled the wagon with her groceries a few steps behind. He set them on the porch. She tipped him, unlocked the door, and carried the bags inside. Shrugged out of her coat and hat, hooked her cane over a chair. Put the cold food in the fridge.

Beatrice had stopped working to eat a sandwich and peeled and cut an apple—passing half of each to Bessie.

"Why, thank you kindly." Jones sat down to eat. Munching on the apple, she stopped, spit out a tooth. "Oh, shit. I'm losing my teeth. I must call the dentist." Upstairs, she heard thumping and bedsprings creaking. "Johns?"

Beatrice nodded. "Lively, too! I've got the downstairs done. Want I should do your bedroom next?"

"Yes, and remind me when you leave to give you a five for the Clorox and Borax. And Bon Ami. Thanks for your help. Oh, and please carry the spuds to the basement. Wait, leave me four on the counter for the stew."

"Yes' um. I best get to it." She stood. Dusted the crumbs off her apron into her hand and tossed them into the trash.

Jones stashed the rest of the groceries into the pantry. Tied on her apron. Cut the roast into chunks, browned them in the kettle. Peeled and chopped the vegetables, scraped them into the pot to add to the stew. Sprinkled salt and pepper over.

Thudding battered the door. She peered out and recognized the men waiting outside. "G' day, councilmen. Have a seat in the parlor. Rose and Joanne should be coming down in a few minutes. Can I offer you a drink?"

"Beers would be good while we wait," the taller one said, tugging at his red tie, the silk knot yielding to his nimble fingers. He folded it and tucked it into his suit pocket.

Bessie pulled two cold bottles of Yuengling out of the fridge, popped the tops.

"Here you go. Keep the change." They each handed her a dollar, settled on the sofa, resuming their conversation.

"Thanks." Bessie strode back in the kitchen to make the girls sandwiches, wrapped them in wax paper, and stuck them in the fridge. Cinnamon wafted her way. She switched off the oven, reached for a roll, and bit down on the yeasty bun. "Hmm. Still warm. Oh, my, that's good."

The phone trilled. She lifted the receiver off the wall phone, stretching the cord to ease down on the chair and finish her roll. "Hello? Bessie Jones. Yessir, you can deliver them tomorrow. Is installment included in the price?" She waited while he answered. "Will you take the old one away too? Good, thank you."

The girls emerged at the head of the stairs. They trooped down, each girl seeing the men to the door and handing Jones two tens. Back in the parlor, they greeted the next johns. Up the stairs, they strode; doors slammed; bedsprings squeaked, and often moans reached the Madam's ears.

The day wore on; the sun slowly sank; darkness shrouded Carlisle as Jones stood sentry at the door. Knocking rapped the door; she let in two soldiers in civvies—regulars—from the War College and offered them drinks. Highballs in hand, they waited until their turn came while the radio played a Burt Bacharach tune.

Jones cocked her head to the side; footsteps thumped on the front porch. The door rattled. "Boy, it's gonna be a busy night." She opened the door to greet her guests.

A stranger held up his badge. "You're busted." He and another officer barged in, knocking the door against the wall. "Get your things, you're under arrest."

"I want my phone call." Bessie sighed, turned the stove off, and stuck the barely warm pot into the fridge. She put the receiver to her ear and dialed her lawyer, Hyman Goldstein.

The second officer climbed the steps two at a time, threw the doors open, catching the couples in the act.

"Get your clothes on; we're hauling you in!" he barked. The handcuffs jingled as he removed them from his utility belt, but one of the men held one hand up—a stop sign.

"That won't be necessary, officer. We'll accompany you willingly."

The young officer nodded. "Come along then. Hurry up, girls, get dressed. You're going to jail."

The next morning, the women, disheveled from their night in jail, stood before Justice of the Peace James D. Griest. Madam Jones waited, her joints aching. Rosemary Jones gripped the table with both hands; Joanne Ellis stood beside her, quaking. Only Goldstein looked fresh and calm in his navy suit.

"Mrs. Bessie Jones, you are charged with operating a house of prostitution and selling liquor without a license. Misses Rosemary Jones and Joanne Ellis, you are charged with prostitution and assignation. How do you plead?"

"They plead not guilty, your honor," replied Goldstein.

"This is not your first appearance before this court," the Justice commented.

"In her defense, I submit that my client runs a fine establishment on a par with venerable traditions such as Molly Pitcher, Jim Thorpe, [and] the Dickinson School of Law."[46]

Assistant D.A. Harold Irwin leaped to his feet. "Objection. I am shocked by the defense attorney's claim that Bessie's House is comparable to Carlisle's most revered institutions! That's outrageous! And the counselor just admitted his client's guilt."

"I insist that Madam Jones runs a respectable business—all neat and clean," Goldstein stated.

Press members scribbled furiously, heads bent over notepads, grinning at the spectacle of the red-faced Irwin facing the implacable Goldstein defending the madam of a brothel.

"So noted," Justice Griest replied. "Be seated." He motioned to the defendants to sit down. He then addressed Irwin. "Call your first witness."

After the policemen testified that they caught the prostitutes in the act, the Justice waved his right hand up. The defendants and Goldstein stood to hear the sentence.

"Mrs. Jones, the court finds you guilty as charged. Bail is set at $500, and you'll pay the court costs. Misses Jones and Ellis, you are found guilty as charged, fined $100 each, and are remanded to the Cumberland County Jail for seven days."

The gavel cracked. "Next."

CHAPTER 13

THE IRS POUNCES

July 1961

While Beatrice stood ironing, using the dining room table as a makeshift board with a towel as a pad, Bessie sliced watermelon in wedges to go with the chicken salad sandwiches in the kitchen. She made the girls' lunch on busy days. "Boy, this is a ripe one." She tasted a sliver, then resumed cutting. You can stay for lunch." She told her maid, laying a fryer on the counter to thaw for supper.

"Okay," Beatrice answered without looking up. "Is that from the farmers' market?"

"It is." Bessie smiled. "I enjoy going to the market. Everythin' fresh and everybody's friendly. You can go with me next time." She nodded at the gladiolas in a tall glass vase centered on the dining room table. "Gittin' to the point basket's too heavy for me to carry."

The phone shrilled. The women jumped, startled.

"Miz Jones."

"Bessie, this is Hymie Goldstein."

"Uh, oh. You sound serious, Mr. G. Bad news?"

"Sorry, ma'am, but the IRS has garnished your bank account again."

"ALL of it?" Her voice climbed an octave. "What for?"

"$191,000. The IRS investigator—a James Mead claims you owe the government for back taxes."

"Can't be! I pay taxes on my employees' salaries and the house!" Her hand trembled.

"What about your income?" he asked. "Did you report it?"

"I'm self-employed."

"Doesn't matter. It's taxable. We don't have much time. The hearing's day after tomorrow; Judge Follmer's presiding. Plus, five other cases are listed on his docket. If you can bring me a record of taxes you paid, receipts, expenses, and any related forms for the past seven years today, I'll look them over, see what we're facing. But this looks serious. This Mead fellow has been inspecting your records for a year."

"Well, I'll be damned," Bessie said, sitting down; the trembling crawled down her legs. "I'll have to look, but I don't have records that go back that far. How can they charge taxes on an illegal income?"

"You have to declare income. You're supposed to save records in case of an audit," Goldstein explained. "Just drop off what you have with my receptionist, and we'll see what's what. Maybe we can plead ignorance of the law."

"Thanks. I'll try. Goodbye." Bessie dropped the receiver in its cradle.

Knock! Knock! Bessie cracked the door open.

A man wearing a black suit, white shirt, and a striped tie handed her a folded paper. "You've been served. Please report to court Thursday, July 30 at ten A.M. Judge Follmer's courtroom." He pivoted on his heels and strode down the sidewalk to his two-toned Chevy.

"What's that all about?" Beatrice asked. The girls and their johns trooped downstairs, money in hand; two more men appeared on the porch. Jones took the bills to the chest, unlocked the drawer, placed $30.00 in it, and locked it. She'd tally the week's total, subtract room and board, and then pay the girls just in case.

"Income taxes," Jones answered. "You can eat lunch, then go home for the day. I have to get ready for court."

"Well, alright, I kin dust and wet-mop tomorrow, I guess." Beatrice turned off the iron, twisted the cord up, and stuck it in the iron's handle; she folded the towel. "I'll just put these away."

"Think I'd be used to goin' to court by now," Bessie mumbled to herself as she lumbered up the stairs, her hands grasping the banister to haul her aging body up. She hung her new black and white dress on the over-the-door hanger in her bedroom. Pulled her walking shoes out of the small closet. Laid out clean underwear. Shuffled to the bathroom to run water in the tub. "Now where did I put those damn tax papers?"

Jones sat in silence as the bailiff called the court to order. "All rise!" as Judge Follmer strode into court, his face stern and posture stiff. His black robe billowed as he mounted the steps to the bench. Taking his seat, he whacked the gavel and called his first case.

The proceedings droned on until the judge smacked the gavel again to signal the next case. The bailiff announced Jones's docket number.

Hyman Goldstein nudged Bessie and stood, the lawyer and the madam. He straightened his tie, took his client's elbow, held the gate open for her, and moved to the far table for defendants. His charcoal suit hugged his tall, athletic frame. They stood before the judge while Follmer made his introductory comments. A deep frown creased his forehead as he read the case notes before him. He glared at the defense table and motioned for all to sit and the Prosecution to begin.

"If it pleases the court," the D.A. stood. " We are charging the defendant, Bessie Jane Jones, with operating a house of prostitution, assignation, and selling beer without a license. The Federal Government's IRS investigator will report that Madam Jones is also charged with income tax evasion and has frozen her bank accounts. I call Investigator James Mead to the stand."

Mead took the witness chair; the prosecutor walked him through his two-year investigation of Jones's finances and bank account records, "I seized $86,000 in her checking and $171,000 in her saving account, the later proceeds coming mainly from gambling in New York."

"Do you have records to substantiate that statement?" the D.A. asked.

"Bank statements. Yes, sir." Mead pointed to the D.A., who walked a sheaf of papers up to the bench and handed them to the judge.

Defense waved aside a cross-examination but stood to explain. "My client has paid $28,000 in back taxes and another $170,000 in penalties, interest, and costs. She seems uncertain why the Federal Government would seize her account. She's unaware that she owed taxes on her income."

"How does your client plead?"

"Not Guilty, your honor."

The judge fumed. "This woman never did an honest day's work in her life. She has appeared before this court numerous times but continues to operate her house of ill repute. And, counselor, I do not accept ignorance of the law as an excuse for avoiding paying income taxes despite the income tax evasion charges last year. Anyone who accumulates $200,000* is no financial neophyte. Will the defendant please stand."[47]

---

* That sum would equal over one million dollars in today's currency.

That remark stung. Bessie murmured to herself, "I work hard."

Standing also, Goldstein added, "May it please the court—"

"No," the judge interrupted. "I'd like to go on record that I'm displeased with counselor's assessment of Madam Jones's establishment as being on par with our revered Molly Pitcher and Jim Thorpe in her 1959 proceedings. Please stand."

"Does the defendant have anything to say in her defense?" the judge turned to Miss Bessie.

"You don't know how I've lived my life. I can turn around and point out at least six or seven clients in this courtroom right now." A weighty silence hypnotized the chambers for a moment as her threat seized everyone's attention.

Follmer cleared his throat and sentenced Jones to one year in federal prison and five years' probation with the possibility of parole. "You are to cease and desist in running a house of prostitution. In addition, the court charges you $3,000 for violating parole from last year's court order."[48]

Goldstein requested leniency considering Jones's health conditions: arthritis, a heart ailment, and poor vision and hearing. The judge countered that the facilities in Muncy could treat her physical ailments. "Report to Muncy Federal Prison on October first."[48]

The gavel banged down like a slammed door.

Bessie descended the stairs of justice, striking out again. Her bank money gone, her joints stiff from sitting so long in one position, she limped home alone with her thoughts, her cane tapping against the sidewalk. She had to pack the meager possessions allowed.

During the three-month interim, Jones outlined to her girls and Beatrice what to do during her absence; she would temporarily close the business in September. She met with Goldstein to set up a bill payment schedule—giving him cash from her pillowcase to cover those expenses. Canceled the newspaper and milk deliveries. Asked a neighbor lady to keep watch over her house.

"Ain't gonna worry about prison," Bessie said, but traveling more than two hours away from home, closing her business, and spending 365 days housed with criminals, maybe murderers—even mental cases—caused many a sleepless night. As she counted down the days, her dread grew.

Two hours in transit blurred Bessie's vision from staring out the window. She stepped into incarnation blindly, shuffling along in handcuffs and ankle restraints. The Muncy State Correctional Institution for Women intimidated; its stately stories a stark reminder of justice. Planted out in the middle of nowhere.

Blinking, she stared at circles of concertina wire topping the fences, its silver-slivered barbs a threat. Acres of ground surrounded the prison's main building, an imposing edifice in this rural setting.

She suffered the indignity of the strip search, her limbs rebelling against the crouch. Her knees cracked; her joints ached.

"Hey, granny, get up," the guard smirked. "Day one."

She grabbed the table's edge and heaved herself up. The prisoner grunted, accepted the drab prison garb, pulling it on as quickly as her arthritic fingers allowed. Picked up her bin of toiletries, trailing the guard along dark hallways through a series of bars and locked doors. Her silence spoke like sound. Entering her cell, her mate sprang off the bottom bunk. "Hiya, old woman, what you in for?"

"Running a house of prostitution."

One consolation: she received a set of false teeth. The prison paroled Bessie eight months later because of ill health. Afterward, she resorted to saving and stashing bills under mattresses. Thousands hid in a pink silk pillowcase in the back of her closet. She cut the pages from a hardback book and hid a stack of fifties in it, carefully sliding it back into the bookcase. Hundreds more went into cigar boxes, which she stuck in the back of her bedroom drawers.

Word spread that Madam Jones had reopened for business, and she no longer visited the bank.

Carlisle hardly noticed renewed activity at Bessie's as the town expanded outward. New businesses moved in. The Wilson School closed; Bellaire School was under construction. The following year, firefighters rushed downtown to douse a fire. The Bowman Department Store was fully engulfed in flames; the roof collapsed, large glass windows exploded, and the fire raged despite the numerous hoses pelting water on the flames. The fire left Kronenberg's as the only large department store operating in downtown Carlisle.

CHAPTER 14

THE NEWCOMERS' SHOCK

June 1963

Constance Morris and Katherine "Kit" Harrison pecked timidly at the front door. Jones opened the door cautiously, looking up and down the dusty street for a vehicle. "May I help you?" Bessie ventured.

The two women, one light-skinned Black with red hair, one pale Caucasian with sandy hair, smiled; the former dressed in a ruffled eyelet crop top, the latter in flowered blouse tied to reveal her midriff. Both wore pedal pushers and sandals, talking at once.

"Good morning, I'm Connie Morris—"

"We're looking for Mrs. Bessie Jones," Kit said. She proffered her hand. "I'm Katherine Harrison, but you can call me Kit."

"Your lucky day. You found her." Bessie smiled.

"We heard about your business. We want to work here."

"Why?"

"Well, we heard the money's good, and you—" Connie began.

"Provide room and board—and furnish our necessities," finished Kit.

The Madam stepped back, gestured for them to enter, pointed to the kitchen table. The comb holding her bun bit into her crown. She adjusted it. The girls eased onto worn kitchen chairs, eyes furtively scanning the room. A window AC unit whirred from the sitting room.

"You're not part of the New Kensington circuit," Jones stated, her coffee eyes looking from one to the other.

They eyed one another, both shaking their heads.

Connie explained, "We work together, but nobody 'handles' us if that's what you mean. We're independent contractors."

"Coffee or tea?" Bessie padded to the stove. "So, no pimp's gonna come rapping at my door, demanding where his girls are and wanting a cut of your pay?"

"Coffee, please. Black," replied Connie. "Uhm, no ma'am; we're a team; we manage ourselves."

"With cream," Kit said. "Thank you." Her hands trembled slightly as she took the cup. "No saucer, please. I can't handle both."

They discussed terms and agreed on a fifty-fifty split.

The Madam pulled the schedule from the top of the fridge. "See, a friend usually delivers two girls, or they arrive by bus every two weeks, work for two or three weeks, and then rotate out to bigger cities like Philly. And I have one part-time girl. So . . ." She tapped the calendar.

"So, can you add us to that list?" Connie leaned over to see the last week of the month clear. She pointed to it. "We can start then."

"Or anytime you say," put in Kit.

Jones's slow smile showed her acceptance. "I like your pluck. Reckon I can slot you in then."

A few weeks later, they became a part of the schedule. On the evening of June 27, 1963, while the girls were entertaining johns, Jones escorted two satisfied men to the front door. "So nice to see you gents again; it's been a while. Come back soon."

"Always a pleasure, ma'am," the younger man nodded, gestured for the older gentleman to precede him out the door.

She let in a stranger who gave the name of a regular to gain entrance. Clean-shaven, young, and fit, he shook his head no as Morris first approached him. She shrugged her shoulders and skirted around him, heading for the kitchen for a drink. Some johns didn't want a Black prostitute, some did. No sweat.

Harrison greeted him in sheer baby doll nightie, smiling. "Hey, stranger, I'm Kit. Come on up. I'll be just a minute." He followed her up the stairs and into the first bedroom. The open window was cracked to catch fitful breezes that eased the stifling heat. In the bathroom across the hall, she filled a basin with warm water, wet a washcloth she'd soaped up, crossed back to the bedroom. "Whatcha need?"

"Why'd you think I'm here? Just the usual."

"Honey, there ain't a usual. Don't you have a preference? Straight intercourse is ten bucks, half 'n half, sixty-nine, and a blow job all fifteen—"

Walking toward him, she noticed he was still fully dressed, except he'd tugged off his polished shoes and tucked something in one. He backed away, the tops of his ears pink.

Kit stopped. "Ah, you're new. I have to wash you. It's Madam's policy." He hesitated, pulling two crisp bills out of his pocket, and laid them down but made no move toward her.

"Half and half then?" She placed the basin on the stand. Then she knew. His crewcut and posture. Those shiny black shoes. Still dressed. Her smile faltered, then dissipated; her stomach clenched. Harrison turned to face a shiny badge thrust before her.

"You're under arrest for prostitution." He reached for her arm.

"Omigod! No, no!" Harrison darted for the window, tugged up the sash, leaning out. Trooper Hunt grabbed her arms, holding her steady while she quaked. "Take it easy. You've never been arrested?"

Kit just shook her head no, her eyes white circles in her face, draining paler than parchment.

"You're not going to faint or jump, are you? Here, sit down. Then get dressed. We're all going downtown."

Madam Jones, Constance Morris, and Katherine Harrison appeared in court before Justice of the Peace Frank Swigert on charges of prostitution and assignation. The JP sentenced Madam Jones to a year in Muncy Prison for Women while the girls were fined $500 apiece for their roles at Bessie's House.[49]

Bessie fumed as they all left the courtroom. "Again? Behind bars with who knows what crazy women—like the one who threw her food, plate and all, into my face. Murderers who shot, knifed, or poisoned their abusive partners, mean as the abuser they killed." Her body shuddered. "Lord, this time, you gave me a mountain I can't climb."

Morris and Harrison tripped lightly down the courthouse steps.

"Whew, no jail time," Kit commented. Connie laughed, her red hair shining in the sunlight and her face tilted toward the sky. Arm in arm, they walked back to 20 Locust Street.

Five months later, President JFK was assassinated. Across the nation, the media focused on the tragedy: the forlorn, stunned widow standing beside LBJ on *Air Force One*. As shocked Americans watched, an army of TV broadcasters described the events. Walter Cronkite removed his glasses and wiped the tears from his eyes while reporting the tragedy. "Everyone's in shock. Vice President Lyndon B. Johnson is being sworn in as president on *Air Force One*." At the funeral, cameras caught John-John saluting his father's casket as the cortège and the riderless horse passed.

Lighting of the eternal flame at Arlington marked the end of the journey.

Controversy surrounded his death. A Warren Commission followed with Pennsylvania senator Arlen Specter advancing the "one-bullet theory." To this day, shadows cast a pall over the young president's assassination as a nation mourned its loss.

Bessie remained at Muncy Prison, stoic but keeping to herself, avoiding the angry ones, the gangs, and the dangerous. She fended most off with a menacing stare.

CHAPTER 15

ADDING INSULT TO INJURY

January 1964

"What's your emergency?"

"Operator, there's a house on fire!" a voice exclaimed.

"What's the address?" the operator responded.

"Twenty East Locust Street. Bessie's house is burning! No one's home. Hurry!" the caller disconnected.

Within minutes, the fire company arrived and doused the flames on the right side of the house and the first floor, soot and smoke blanketing the charred furniture, heat melting the records on the turntable, the flames destroying all they touched. Fire chief Ray Kelley dialed state police, requesting an inspector. "Looks like the place has been vandalized." He paused to listen. "No, no one's in residence, but we found the owner's sister in the basement. A neighbor reported that Madam Jones is in prison, so the house was supposedly empty. The stairs and second floor are intact, so the structure's sound. Yes, I'll wait."

A tall man in a dark suit and black-framed glasses stood in the doorway. "I'm Hyman Goldstein, Madam Jones's lawyer. What's going on here?" His eyes roamed around the blackened remains. "Oh, no!"

"Someone set the house on fire," Kelley responded. "We found accelerant on the couch, so that's the source. Sister's in the basement. Seems disoriented. We can't get her to come out. Since the fire's out, I didn't want to make a scene by having my men forcibly evict her."

"May I?" Goldstein nodded toward the basement steps. He hurried to the kitchen sink first and dampened his handkerchief under the faucet.

Kelley nodded. "Be my guest."

Downstairs, a coughing and teary-eyed Marion Middleton wandered the perimeter, peering in and under stacked boxes, rusty screens, an old rocking horse, and other detritus shunted into permanent storage. Shelves on one end boasted home-canned green beans, tomatoes, and peaches, their vibrant colors beaming from Mason jars.

"Marion, what are you doing here?" he asked gently.

"Looking for my new shoes." Her hands felt along dusty shelves, knocking over knickknacks stored there. She peered into a box of Christmas decorations. Dust motes swirled; the air tasted charred and smelled like burnt plastic.

"Come, take my hand; I'll guide you out," Goldstein offered.

"Bessie's gone! I need my shoes!" Tears streamed down her face, her hair a nest of tangles. Dirt and coffee splotched her housedress.

"You can't stay here; it's not safe! Someone set the house on fire. Firemen put it out, but hot spots may flare up again. The first floor is ruined. Come on. We'll find you a place to stay. You can buy new shoes."

She jerked her hand away, wiping her burning eyes. "I'm not staying with strange Negrahs!"[50]

"Want to go to the hospital then? You've inhaled smoke, and who knows what chemicals that plastic contains." Goldstein reached for her hand. This time she acquiesced and let the lawyer guide her up the stairs.

Police Chief Edward Still stopped them. "Did you start this fire?" he asked Middleton. "Let me see your hands." She smelled like smoke, not gasoline.

She shook her head. "No! Bessie's my sister. Why would I do that? Who'd do this to her? She's kind to everyone!" Then both hands shot up, palms out, and then gestured at the destruction. "This is her life! Her business! Her house!"

"Where is she?" The chief asked.

"In Muncy State Prison for Women," Goldstein volunteered, guiding Middleton out the door. To Still, he said, "You can get Marion's statement later."

Police arrived and canvassed the domicile. Upstairs, clothes and other belongings had been dumped and scattered. Chief Still stood surveying the wreckage on the first floor. "This smells like an inside job, an arson to cover the robbery. I have a hunch."

He sent his men down the lane to 24 East Locust Street to question Frank Stackfield, an acquaintance of Jones. The man returned to Bessie's place, nodding to Still, looking sheepish. "Yeah, we knew Bessie's in jail, so we helped ourselves to some of her cash. She has plenty." He led them to Jones's bedroom closet, disappeared, then backed out, holding a pink pillowcase containing about $43,600.[51] Police confiscated and took custody of the cash.

"Who's we?" demanded Still. Stackfield led him to 24 East Locust, Marion's house, where Ralph Taylor Conn and Beatrice (Ahl) Gibson waited.

"Search him," Still ordered his officer, who found $5,600 on Stackfield and $520 on Gibson.

The trio was arrested for stealing, Gibson for arson, arraigned, and bound over for trial.

In court, Judge Dale Shughart presided over the case. The D.A. put Chief Still and Fire Chief Kelley on the stand to describe

Police standing behind confiscated money. (Courtesy of the Cumberland County Historical Soceity.)

the crime scene. "One of my men found the gas can in the old outhouse."

Then Stackfield mounted the witness box slowly. "We knew the house was empty," he said. "So, we been borrowin' money from Bessie while she gone."

"Borrowing? Since when?" the Judge inquired.

"January." The man had enough sense to bow his head.

Gibson also confessed, "I was intoxicated and did not realize what I was doing. I did not mean to set the house on fire." The judge sentenced her from eleven to twenty-three months in county prison for arson and robbery. The men were sentenced for theft separately.[52]

After eight months, Jones was paroled. She called Castle's to replace the burned floor and walls, Billet's Electric to rewire the first floor, and found lamps and end tables at the antique stores. At the second-hand furniture shop, she found a like-new sofa.

Marion helped, teasing her sister, "You can afford to buy new furniture."

Bessie shook her head. "Don't have that much money now; feds took it. Besides, I want a comfortable, lived-in look. Oh, and look at that China cabinet. It's like Mama's. I'll take that, too." She pointed to the one with glass doors and curved legs. "Would you please deliver these to 20 East Locust?" The man nodded while tallying up her bill.

The arson and robbery garnered intense scrutiny from the authorities, specifically the IRS. Their agents and the Carlisle legal team representing Jones, the fire department, police, and sheriff's offices all claimed the money. The Feds won.

In Carlisle in 1966, the federal government seized "$192,000 from Bessie's savings account to apply to her back taxes, and she spent a few months in a federal penitentiary in West Virginia."[53]

Another tragedy struck Bessie that year also; her brother William, her closest sibling, died. The funeral was brief; she grieved his loss as his body was laid to rest near their mother's and sister's gravesites. His marker listed his name, service in WWI, and his birth and death dates, 1895-1966.[54.] Not much to show for a life. She'd miss his help in running errands, fixing dings and clogs at the house, trekking to the New York races, running interference for her when needed. She sighed. "Now you rest, brother."

For the next two years, business at Bessie's Place followed the Madam's routine, the seasons slipping by, Carlislers' attention turning to school and football in the Fall. Snow and cold ushered in winter. After celebrating Thanksgiving, shoppers hustled in and out of stores for Christmas gifts and, weeks later, welcomed in the New Year. On Valentine's Day, children traded greetings at school, excited by the ones dropped in their paper bags decorated with hearts. Gale-force winds downed some trees in March. April and May were tardy that year. Tulips and crocuses braved the chill, poking their heads into the air. June sparkled with jeweled grass and flowering gems like red roses and purple petunias. Apple blossoms scented the air. Children burst from school for another summer vacation.

Two by twos, scantily clad prostitutes arrived and left according to the Madam's timetable. No police officers swooped down for the duration.

CHAPTER 16

THE SUMMER OF 1968

An undercurrent of unease eddied through the quaint town, its adults anxious and worried. Nineteen sixty-eight signaled 'America's loss of innocence,' claimed the experts. On-site broadcasters reported the ugly destruction on TV: the rat-a-tat-tat of machine guns, Huey copters thundering overhead, soldiers in woodland green wrestling through the jungle with leaves plastered to their helmets—bringing the devastation into American living rooms and splashing explicit photos across national newspapers and magazines.

No one wanted to talk of the unpopular Viet Nam Conflict, the war that ignited protests across college campuses. The more soldiers President Johnson and the Pentagon sent, the louder the protests grew. The Viet Cong's successful Tet Offensive indicated that the conflict was unwinnable. As it escalated, the president's ratings fell. Eventually, 58,000 American servicemen and women lost their lives as protest songs urged politicians to "make peace, not war."

Presidential candidate Robert F. Kennedy fell to an assassin's bullet while campaigning in California. Civil Rights advocate Dr. Martin Luther King, who wanted his "children to grow up in an America where they'd be judged by the content of their character rather than the color of their skin," was assassinated on the balcony of his hotel room. The death of the eloquent and popular leader left a gaping hole in the Civil Rights Movement, although others like the Reverend Jesse Jackson and John Lewis stepped into the gap to soldier on. A cloud of collective despair gathered over a mourning nation as newspapers and broadcasters reported the tragedies.

In the nation that year, two radical organizations sprang from the turbulence of that era: The Black Panthers, a militant and outspoken group that worked to improve the plight of African Americans in the California ghettos, and The National Organization for Women. Carlisle, however, was far removed from California or race riots that besieged the cities.

Betty Friedan's *Feminine Mystique* gave voice to the discontent educated American housewives faced in their defined role as housewives and mothers. Academics and activists like Gloria Steinem, who co-founded *Ms.* magazine, became the leading voice of the feminist movement. Steinem addressed American women in a speech urging reform: "There is no simple reform. Sex and race are easy because they are visible differences of the primary ways of organizing human beings into superior and inferior groups and into cheap labor upon which this system still depends."[55] The National Organization for Women gained steam by advocating women's issues like supporting the Equal Rights Amendment and women's reproductive freedom.

Housewives satisfied with their status as homemakers clashed with feminists. That divide would foment and fracture women into two factions: those who worked full-time outside the house and the stay-at-home moms.

Added to the tumult caused by the Viet Nam conflict, President JFK's assassination, its attendant conspiracy theories, and race riots, the sixties signified the flux, unrest, and turmoil that racked the nation. The American myth of Camelot ended, ushering in an age of cynicism.

CHAPTER 17

THE MULE

1968

Trees fully dressed in leafy green, and flowers burst with color in window boxes along the downtown Carlisle streets. Pedestrians ambled along, ducking in the shops, stopping awhile at Bosler's Memorial Library checking out books and enjoying the summer. Dickinson College students had scattered after their semester's end. Teens scooped frozen custard at Massey's; businessmen stopped for lunch at various eateries—a quick Texas wiener or a more leisurely sandwich and fries at the Hamilton.

Carlisle citizens were enjoying a day at the fair. The fairgrounds bustled where men were setting up the stage for the Vogues that evening. Lunch wagons hawked hot dogs and burgers, and food vendors offered caramel popcorn, cotton candy, French fries, and funnel cakes. An ice cream truck sold popsicles, creamsicles, and Eskimo pies. Canvas tents housed games like toss the ping-pong ball, win a goldfish; shooting targets featured revolving ducks with prizes like stuffed animals; slingshots, jump ropes, or paddle balls.

"Get your fresh, ice-cold lemonade!" barked a white-haired man at one stand while his partner squeezed lemons, her arms jiggling with the twisting. "Only fifty cents!"

"Step right up. Take a chance. Win a prize," another offered.

Dads and kids loitered at the games, dithering over which ones to play. Women headed for the baked goods to see who won prizes for the best cake, pie, or fudge. Everyone wanted to see the fresh produce ribbon winners.

Neighbors greeted one another. Kids streaked around the guy ropes anchoring the canvas canopies, meeting friends they hadn't seen since school let out. High school students loitered in the parking lot, leaning on cars, smoking cigarettes. They listened to the top forty hits blaring from car radios, including Presley's "Suspicious Minds," Franklin's "Chain of Fools," and the Supremes' "Love Child," among others. High school seniors sought dates to Haar's drive-in to see *2001: A Space Odyssey* and hoping to get lucky during the second feature.

At the fairgrounds, Madam Bessie Jones, dressed in the floppy straw hat, leaned on her cane, and walked along the rows with her sister Marion and two of her girls, Georgia Schneider and another prostitute, dressed in sleeveless tops tied at the waist and shorts, their feet clad in flipflops. Jones bought them all lemonade and hot dogs, plus peanut butter fudge to take home. As the sun traveled westward, the Madam glanced at her watch, switching her cane to her other hand.

A beefy man dressed in khaki standing behind the shooting gallery canopy holding a beer stumbled toward them. "You filthy, fuckin' whores need to crawl back to your cage. Better yet, get lost; leave town. The good citizens of Carlisle don't want you here." He swilled down the rest of the bottle. Tossed it aside. Spit toward them.

Georgia pivoted to retort, her hands fisted, ready for a fight. "Look, asshole—"

Jones grabbed her arm and propelled her toward the parking lot. "Silence is safety."

"I'm not afraid of the rube." Schneider clenched her teeth but let Jones guide her along.

"He's drunk, and we need to keep a low profile. Don't need scuffles with the police. Time to go, girls. We don't want to keep anyone waiting in line on such a hot day, or our money will walk away."

The younger one protested, "We want to stay for the concert, and we haven't seen the tents at the back." She pointed back.

"You're not missing a thing. The carnies perform a sleazy strip tease for men to gawk and whistle," Jones noted.

"I've heard they let men feel them up for a few dollars more." Marion shook her head. "Anyway, you can't go to tonight's concert unless you can find substitutes. Bess and I are way too old, have too much mileage, for practicing this profession." She tossed the paper and napkin into a near-by trash barrel and aimed for her car. She glanced at Schneider. "You have to excuse drunks."

Georgia nodded. The girls giggled at the thought of two old women engaging in sex.

"Poor Minnie's holding the fort by herself," Jones added. She lumbered toward the '64 Impala, settling herself in the passenger's seat. "Boy, the seat's mighty warm, sister." The other two climbed into the backseat.

"Sorry, all the shade was taken when we got here." She reversed, backing the car off the grass onto the gravel driveway, the Chevy rocking gently as she changed gears, turned, and headed toward town. When Marion turned down Locust Street, no parking places were available along the curb. "I'll have to let you out here," she said, stopping behind a carload of teenage boys.

"Thanks for the ride," Bessie said; the girls hopped out of the back and, seeing the queue, skedaddled inside. "What are y'all doin' here?" she asked the driver, who was wearing a Big Spring t-shirt.[56]

"We've come to Bessie's," the teen said, his smile wide and charming. The one in the passenger's seat glanced at her, then quickly away, his eyes darting over the shabby dwelling and the waiting men. "We want one of your girls for graduation. How much?"

Madam Jones adjusted her glasses. "Now, you boys are kind to stop by, but you're too young. Come back when you're grown. Why don't you go to the Fair instead? Enjoy the concert. Drive safely. Bye, now." She turned away, nodded at the men in line, and opened the door. "Why don't the next four come on in? Can I get you a drink while you wait?" she asked the others, each nodding and giving her their preferences, whiskey or beer.

Once inside, she laid the candy on the kitchen counter and looped her cane on a hook. She poured the drinks, carried them outside on a tray, and collected the patrons' money. "Won't be long. Thank you for waiting." She smiled at each.

In the parlor, she stacked forty-five records—Otis Redding, Marvin Gay's "You're All I Need" and Percy Sledge's "It's All Wrong But It's All Right" on the spindle, turning the player on. The arm automatically swung over, settling in the groove. "Sitting on the dock of the bay . . ." Redding sang, his voice stretching time at summer's ease.

Minnie descended the steps, handing Jones a fistful of tens. Her sheer nightie revealed full breasts, slim waist, and ample hips. "I'll be leaving after this set. I'm knackered." Sashaying to the parlor arch, she beckoned. "Anyone coming my way?" She chuckled at her pun. A sunbaked farmer dusted his overalls and stood to follow her upstairs. The madam eased into the chair to entertain a burly, barrel-chested businessman until one of the girls was free.

Schneider joined them at the table and smiled at the stranger. "Hey, Mister. What's your name?"

"They call me Mule." He smiled at her and nodded up the stairs.

"Why?"

"Let's say I'm hung." He winked. Wanna find out?"

"I don't believe you!" She stood, ready for a challenge, and they climbed the stairs.

Hearing a commotion upstairs followed by Schneider's scream, Jones grabbed the broom and climbed up to the first bedroom, barging into the room.

The john was straddling Schneider, trying to force his erect penis into her. She cried, "Stop! It doesn't fit! It hurts!" Both her fists pummeled his massive chest. "You're hurting me!"

Bessie grabbed his arm, pulling him back and yelling, "Back off, Mule!" She whacked his head and shoulders with the handle. "Get your clothes, get outta here! Never come back! Or I'll call the police!"

Surprisingly, he complied, backing away and rubbing his head, more stunned than angry.

"Are you alright?" the Madam asked, her hands patting Georgia's bare back, red marks blooming on her shoulders. "Let me get some Vicks for these bruises." She crossed over into her bedroom, swiped the Vicks off the nightstand, and returned to minister to her girl's bruises.

"Th-Thanks!" Georgia gulped air, crossed her arms over her stomach. "Th-thanks. I'm done for the day . . . I'm sore. Hope I'm not bleeding."

"Let me see. No blood. That's good. OK, you rest now. We'll wash your sheets later."

Downstairs, Mule shouldered the door open, lurched out, trying to zip his fly. He fished his car keys out of his jeans pocket and climbed in the hot car. "What I need is a cold beer and a hot chick." Pulling away from the curb, he aimed the car toward the

Carlisle Fairgrounds. "Those damn uppity Jones's spinners! I'll get some action from the strippers."

CHAPTER 18

TRICKED AGAIN

June 29, 1968

Sue Ann Morgan and Donna Marie Fisher descended the bus steps onto hot macadam, the heat rippling from the surface. One carried a tote, the other an over-sized quilted hobo bag. Carlisle streets remained quiet on Saturday morning, save for the Farmer's Market on the square. Murmured conversation reached their ears. Dressed in shorts and cropped, tie-dyed tees with their feet clad in sandals, they strode down the alley to Bessie's and hurried up the crumbling concrete steps.

The Madam let them in. "Good mornin' girls. Have a good trip?"

"Well, I played solitaire." Morgan shrugged as if the heat had sapped her energy. "We took the red-eye to get here on time."

"I read to pass the time, but the story isn't holding my interest." Fisher waved the paperback romance.

"Why's that?" Morgan looked at the book jacket: a curvaceous woman with a mane of auburn waves lay against a bare-chested, athletic cowboy with black wavy hair, striking features, and six-pack abs.

"The woman can't seem to live without a man." Fisher pulled a grin as she waved the novel for all to see.

"That ain't just any man, sister," Morgan said, gesturing at the gaudy cover.

Fisher shrugged and stuffed the romance into her bag.

"Want anything to eat?" Bessie paused in the doorway as the girls aimed for the stairs. "Coffee?"

"No, thanks. We'll settle in." Morgan observed, fanning herself. "Think I'm gonna take a bath. I can smell the heat rising off me."

"Iced tea would be lovely if you have some," Fisher said. "You called us in a day early."

"Yes, one of the girls was injured; my part-timer quit to get married. Don't that beat all: she said she wanted to work to avoid marriage." She lifted a shoulder.

"Guess she changed her mind." Morgan wound and clipped her coffee hair with caramel highlights up into a hasty French twist, peeling off clothes as she climbed the stairs. Fisher followed but continued up the second flight of stairs to the stifling attic to unload her belongings.

"I'll just freshen up at the sink." Fisher flipped a headband over her head that pushed her bangs off her face. Splashed cool water from the pitcher on the dresser over her freckled face and arms, washing from the neck down as not to disturb her make-up. Patted gently with a dry cloth. No time to reapply base, eyeliner, blush, or pencil in eyebrows again.

Morgan stepped into three inches of tepid water. She soaped up, rinsed off, and toweled down in record time, and then unclipped her hair, finger-combed it loosely, let it fall naturally to her shoulders.

"We open in an hour," Jones called up after them.

"We'll be down in a jiff," Fisher called down, muttering. "Good thing we make good money," she commented in an aside to her companion. She pulled out a chartreuse satin negligee and let it fall over her head and curl around her curves. She slipped her feet into mules and whisked her drink from the kitchen table, easing quickly into the parlor and perched on the armchair, leaving the sofa for the johns.

Morgan decided on a red kimono that complemented her olive complexion, leaving an inch gap to her navel and tying the silk sash loosely around her waist. Morgan joined Fisher, a half-smile pulling at her painted lips. "Looking good, though you might want to lose the headband."

"Oops, I forgot. Thanks." Fisher nodded, her mules barely clinging to her toes. She stretched it and lifted it, wrapped it around her glass. Swiped her bangs down. "You too. Adore your highlights; they look natural." She sipped the cold tea laced with lemonade, the ice, and pulp swirling in the glass. "Mmm. This is delicious."

Rapping struck the door as the clock chimed ten. "Right on time." The day began, the prostitutes' routine practiced and honed to precision. Gents at the door. Jones ushered them to the parlor and offered a drink. The girls greeted them and escorted them upstairs. Bedsprings squeaked. Fifteen minutes later, men left smiling. The clock had just chimed eleven o'clock when Madam Jones opened the door. She admitted a regular, who stopped long enough to grab Morgan's hand, and together they trooped upstairs.

Another pair dressed in jeans and flannel shirts over tees mounted the step to the porch. Though she didn't recognize these two, they said they came from the Carlisle Pike truck stop. The madam nodded and admitted them. Their ploy worked.

Trooper Charles McBreen and Corporal Paul Petzar observed a woman in red traipse down the stairs, hand Jones money, jotted a note in a folder, and returned to the john upstairs. Jones stuck the bills in a strongbox bolted to the drawer in the dining room.

"Would you men like a beer or a shot of Jack Daniels?" Bessie smiled as they settled on the sofa.

They shook their heads. "We're good."

Fisher waltzed over, hand on her hip, and asked, "Which one of you gents want to go first?" She smiled and extended her hand. Though dressed like long-haulers, the men smelled fresh; their jeans and shirts clean—not spotted with grease, coffee, or ketchup.

Petzar stood up, took her hand, winked. "Let's get to it!" Up the stairs they went. The undercover officer started undressing, shedding his shoes and shirt. Fisher left him to get a basin of soapy water, taking it back to the second bedroom, as Morgan was still occupied in the first room. She looked up at Petzar, noting a scar running along his chin. She stopped, set the basin down.

He waved his badge at her. "You're under arrest for prostitution. Get dressed. Let's go. She skirted around him, swearing under her breath. Opening the first bedroom door, Morgan noted the two coupled, the john thrusting.

"Hey, Sue Ann. We've been pinched. Get dressed."[57]

The guy turned his head and stopped, groping for his boxers and pants to cover his nakedness, his face as red as his sunburned neck.

The four clambered down the steps.

Jones's hand tightened on the doorknob, her legs tired and swollen from the long day on her feet. She watched the cops wrest the strongbox from the drawer, prying it free and confiscating the money. "I want to call my lawyer." She grabbed her purse from the kitchen counter.

"Go ahead. He can meet us at the station. We're arresting the men too," Petzar told McBreen.

Jones whispered to herself. "Damnation. I can't catch a break. Bet they'll send me to Muncy again." She dialed Goldstein's home phone number and dipped into her emergency fund from the honeypot on the fridge.

At the July courtroom two weeks later, the girls were fined and released for time served. Madam Jones posted $500 bail and walked home alone, the cane tapping along. She cursed herself for falling for the cops' trick but sighed, thankful the judge didn't send her away this time. "I'd get down on my knees, Lord but can't do that anymore."

CHAPTER 19

"THE BELL TOLLS FOR THEE"

October 1971

The sun smiled warmth, but the air chilled the bones. On her way to church, Bessie could hear the bells tolling the hour; the churches across town—all chiming harmoniously, the music beckoned, calming and echoing across town. She took her seat, helloing neighbors, and church members along the aisle.

"Welcome to Sunday morning worship on this beautiful sunny day," the Presbyterian minister addressed his congregation. "Today, we have a guest from the Baptist Church in Lexington, Kentucky, Dr. John Payne, for our mission week. His sermon will be on *For Whom the Bell Tolls*. For our Bible reading, please turn to Romans 12:18. He paused as Bible pages whispered to Romans, "If it be possible, as much as lieth within you, live peaceably with all men." And Revelation 1:03, "Blessed is he that readeth, and they that hear the words of this prophecy, and keep those things that are written therein, for the time is now at hand."

"Please stand. Join the choir in "Love Lifted Me.""

"I was sinking deep in sin," the congregation's voices rose and fell until they reached the refrain and harmonized.

The visiting preacher wore a pale grey suit, white shirt, and black and yellow striped tie. Bald on top, a grey fringe ringed his head; he adjusted his horn-rimmed bifocals. He motioned people to sit down and thanked them for inviting him to their house of worship. He laid his Bible on the podium with several slips of paper. "Live peacefully with all. The time is at hand. How true as we watch as the war wages on the news in our living rooms, little boys reenacting the fighting with army figures. To make them even more realistic, my son dabbed red paint on his. We cannot seem to learn from history. Plus, riots spawn in the streets. We hear neighbors argue with neighbors and read about families torn apart from dissent and drugs.

"Our younger generation has a valid point: They say, 'Make peace, not war.' Turn on the TVs and radios; listen to their pro-test songs. 'How long will it take 'til we learn?' We see the flag-draped coffins unloaded from cargo planes. Only the dead and wounded understand the true price of freedom. Yes, even those of us who returned from that Hell on Earth called World War II are wounded by our memories—plagued by nightmares. We're the walking wounded if we're lucky!

"See the divide among different ethnicities of the human race as African Americans march against injustice, especially the Jim Crow laws a yoke around their necks. Their leader cut down in his prime last April. Listen to the pundits brandishing their doomsday opinions."

"Amen!"

"But all is not lost. I am reminded of John Donne, a famous British minister and poet, who also wrote meditations. In Medi-tation Seventeen, he writes about our connections, that if we lose one life, we all feel the effect. He compares us"—the preacher pointed to the congregation and then to himself—"to land. If a piece breaks off, it affects us all. We've lost thousands of soldiers overseas. Each year, we lose thousands to diseases and accidents. And how many thousands to violence here and abroad? Donne concludes his essay, 'Never send to know for whom the bell tolls; it tolls for thee.'

"I see you're nodding. The words are familiar because Ernest Hemingway wrote a book titled *For Whom the Bell Tolls* about an American named Robert Jordan who joins the resistance in Spain to blow up a bridge; one theme conveys his courage under fire because he faces certain death. Another points to the coward's reaction to war. Other readers mention his love for Marie. That should be our focus too.

"So much for 'live peaceably with all men.' Love one another because the time is at hand. Don't wait for tomorrow." As he warmed to his sermon, his cadence rising and falling, Bessie nodded off and dozed until roused by the closing hymn. The congregation rose as one—comfortable with the ritual of worship. Rituals are our talisman against the darkness we hold at bay until we must embrace it.

Madam Jones wended her way home, her cane tapping a tune on the sidewalk. "Thank God it's Sunday 'cause I'm getting mighty tired." With each step, her arthritic joints in her knees crackled and popped. Again, the church bells tolled the hour. "Preacher said the bells tolling means . . ."

Sandy Jackson was preparing dinner. Fried chicken, collard greens with a ham hock, and baked potatoes. Jones's niece had dropped off a pan of apple crisp at the house before church. "Connie took the bus to Harrisburg already. How was the sermon?" Jackson emerged from the kitchen, an apron tied over her t-shirt and jeans. Blonde waves framed a comely face with wide brown eyes and pert nose, and generous lips.

"Lovely. A visiting minister, Dr. John preached on bells tolling, war, peace, and love."

"Too bad people can't live that way. You don't see a lot of peace and love nowadays. Just grab and gimme. What about the bells?"

"They mean time's passing. Don't wait for the end to repent." Bessie removed her hat and gloves. Leaned her cane in the corner.

"Oh. I thought the bells were calling people to church." Sandy used tongs to lift the golden chicken pieces out of the bubbling Crisco and drained them on paper towels. She turned off the heat. "I always liked the church potluck dinners the most: BBQ meatballs, potato salad, Jell-O, and my mom'd make a bundt cake or fruit cobbler. Our Preacher always made homemade ice cream."

"I have to take off my Sunday best." Bessie smiled, remembering Mama's insistence that her kids save their best dresses and shoes for Sundays. She hung the nubby beige coatdress on a hanger over her closet with the other dresses sheathed in plastic. Sighing, she laid her book and glasses on her bedside chair, sliding the pillowcases aside. The memory of Mama pulling the little ones in the red wagon to church while Al, Willie and Bessie trotted along beside floated across her mental screen. "Mama bought it at Bixler's; we took the one on display 'cause it was already put together," she reminisced aloud.

She dropped to the bed to roll her nylons off and laid them on the chair. "Time to change your bed." Tugging off the top and fitted sheets, Jones left a quilt at the bottom of the bed. Gazing about the small bedroom, she noticed the dresser cluttered with a can and bottles of Lysol and Listerine with a round pan with a scoop in a worn dishpan beside. A shawl was draped over a corner of the mirror. A basket of paper and boxes leaned against the dresser.[58] "I'll tidy up later. Need to eat first."

She pulled an everyday shift over her head, tugged it over her hips. Pushed her black-framed glasses to the bridge of her nose and hobbled downstairs, the fragrant scents luring her to the kitchen for quiet dinner with Sandy.

The night temperatures dropped, cooling Carlisle's sidewalks off. Sugar leeched from the maple and oak leaves, their last days a burst of crimson, gold, and rust. Dry wind-swept leaves scuttled into the street and onto the front porch, where they were captured by the railing. Jones sniffed the mustiness of burning leaves a ways off. At 9:30 pm, soft rapping tapped the back door—a thump and bump like someone stumbling. Slowly, Jones cracked it open. Did a bird fly into a window? She stepped outside, glancing up and down the lane.

Nobody there.

CHAPTER 20

LIKE A THIEF IN THE NIGHT

September 30, 1972

In August, the Washington Redskins honed their skills at football camp on Dickinson's practice field before the NFL season, the "huh" grunts of linemen pushing sleds across the fields. Crowds gathered along the fence to watch, savoring their frozen custard. When the Redskins left town, Fall whisked into Carlisle once again, the leaves whispering in the breeze. Residents welcomed the cooler nights as they shrugged off summer and sent the children back to school. The high school band practiced after school, the clack of the drums keeping time to marching feet. Teen athletes donned helmets and practiced football plays, hoping for a winning season. Cars lining Main and College Streets signaled the Dickinson College Fall Semester in full swing.

At 20 East Locust, the day began with going to church, dinner at noon, and preparations for the week. Laundry and ironing followed, then totaling the week's accounts. Jones jotted down a grocery list. Dusk lingered. Too soon, the sun dipped beyond the horizon. Then darkness stole the stage. Jackson pattered around upstairs, footsteps padded along the stairs, then she entered the bathroom. Water dribbled into the tub. Later, the water gurgled down the drain when she unplugged the tub stopper.

Madam Jones dragged her body up the stairs, crawling up the last five. Arthritic pain hampered her movements, her body demanding she slow down, her limbs swollen and tight. Footfalls tapped downstairs; urgent whispers rose to Madam Jones. Dropping heavily on the mattress, she shook her head at the sight of the clutter, with folded sheets and fabric on the chair next to her bed. Her shawl draped over the corner of the mirror.

Rapping at her bedroom door, Jackson poked her head in. "Steve brought Georgia."

Madam's brows knit; she sighed. Using her cane to push herself up and hobble downstairs once more, she met them at the door. "What's goin' on?"

The bulky Black man from New Kensington took off his hat. "Geor-ja wants to stop 'ere. She sick. Bit loopy from drinkin', my guess."

"What's she doing here? This isn't her week." Bessie frowned.

"Uhm. Says she needs work. And she's pregnant. Goin' home but wants to spend the night here." He set Schneider's purse and a valise down inside the door.

"Alright. Sandy, take her upstairs; put her to bed. See if she wants some Ginger ale and crackers to settle her stomach." Bessie stood aside. Sandy scooped up the bags; Georgia drooped against Sandy as they mounted the stairs.

"Mighty kind of you; thanks." Jones handed him a twenty. The driver turned to go as she eased the door shut, shaking her head. "Got herself knocked up."

"Might as well do these while they settle." She rinsed the glasses and set them to drain as energy drained from her. At 1:30 A.M., Bessie trudged up the stairs, gripping the banister arm over arm, lugging her septuagenarian body along. She undressed. Pulling a nightgown over her slip, she tissued off her makeup and washed her face. Laid the green and white washcloth over the basin. With fingers splayed, she placed a hairnet over her hair, turned to look at her bare mattress, and sighed.

She heard the girls whispering.

The folded, clean sheets reprimanded her, but she was too tired to make the bed. "Tomorrow." Footsteps descended. Did the front door open and shut? Slipping on her robe in case she had to answer the door again, she sat on her bed to rub liniment onto her swollen legs. Picking up her devotional booklet, she paged through it while the minutes ticked away, her eyes drooping, the words blurring.

Her bedroom door flew open, an assailant brandishing a knife. "I want your money." The knife waved toward the closet, but Bessie barred the way. The knife darted toward her; Jones circled away.

"Why are you robbing me? No! Get out of my house before I call the police." She lurched for her phone—no dial tone. "You cut my outside line? Why? Help! Sandy, are you there?" Silence.

Her assailant's hand snaked out, the knife bit into her arm. The sting registered a moment later. Bessie fought, slapping, scratching, and smacking, trying to dislodge the knife from an angry hand, darting and dodging. It struck a second time; pain ripped through her torso. One hand tried to stem the river of blood soaking her clothes. Still, she flailed at her attacker—a third strike. The assailant shoved the washcloth in her victim's mouth. Jones toppled across the bed, heard the thief rummaging in the closet, and then lost consciousness. She bled out. Taking one of the stockings, the killer pulled the body's right hand back and crossed it over the left. Ducking into the closet, the killer grabbed a pillowcase, stuffing handfuls of cash in a carryall.

Footsteps pounded downstairs, quaking hands grabbed the Preference and receipt books and scrambled out the back door, slamming and locking it. The killer wiped the knife, threw it into the backyard, hurried down the lane, tugged off the gloves, and tossed them into a smoldering leaf barrel.

Had to get away. How to get away? The killer hurried down the alley toward Western Auto as a cab pulled alongside. Hailing it, the indoor light revealed an occupant: Sandy! "What are you doing here? Where were you?"

"Star Lite Motel. What's the matter? Get in. You're shaking like a leaf," Sandy ordered.

"We need to call the police, no, an ambulance. I can't get in. The place is locked up."

The cab driver, John Bubb, climbed out of the cab and tried the door, and then sprinted around back to check that one too.

He returned to the cab. "Can't raise anyone. Back in the cab, he asked, "Don't you have a key? They may be sleepin' inside. I'm not waking up people inside without good reason."

"No, then let's go. Take me back to the motel," Sandy directed.

"I need to go to Pittsburgh," the second one said.

"I'm ending my shift. I'm local, can't drive that far. Put in fifteen hours already." He drove away, retracing his path to the motel, shaking his head. He dropped Jackson off. "Look, I can drive you to Harrisburg, where you can get a taxi to Pittsburgh."

"How much would that cost?"

"Plenty. 'Bout $100 with $10 turnpike fee." Calling ahead, he requested a driver. He drove north until he reached Harrisburg. The customer gave him a twenty. "Thanks."

CHAPTER 21

THE CHASE

Cruising through Carlisle, Trooper Michael Brennan got the call. "I'm on it. Ten-four." Minutes later, he drove up the ramp to the Turnpike, flicked on the lights clearing a path—heading west. He accelerated until the vehicle hit seventy. A black and white followed, lights whirring and siren whining. He picked up his radio: "Cut the siren." It silenced. Few vehicles dotted the road, so the officers barreled on. Roughly twelve minutes later, he pulled over a taxi, checked the license plate. Unsnapped his holster, drew his gun, held his flashlight and weapon at eye level as he approached. "Get out of the vehicle!" he barked.

The b&w pulled up behind the taxi and disgorged Officer Isaac Black and his partner, their pistols drawn and aimed. Two more state troopers blocked the road at either end, jumping out and kneeling on the macadam behind their open doors, pistols aiming at the taxi.

The cab driver emerged, turned, placed his hands on the taxi's roof; he knew the drill. Brennan opened the back door. Out climbed a woman in her thirties—blonde hair with dark roots wearing a brown coat, white sweater over pants that gaped open, revealing a swollen abdomen. She slung a purse over her shoulder and hauled out an overnight bag.

The officer noticed money stuffed in her pants. "Turn around." He unhooked his handcuffs and snapped them around her left wrist, then her right. "You are under arrest for robbery and leaving the scene of a crime. You have the right to remain silent . . ." He Mirandized her, walked the woman back to the patrol car, opened the back door. Guided her head under the doorframe, shut the door.

"Follow me," he ordered the cabbie. Once he reached the Newville Substation, he called it in. "I apprehended a woman in a cab matching the BOLO with money stuffed in her pants, purse, and valise. Yes, the cabdriver's here too." Brennan listened to the detective. "Murder? Yes, sir. I'll book her and print her and then escort her to the Carlisle jail. Yes, sir."

He interviewed the cabbie being held in a separate interrogation room. "What's your name?"

"Art Etnoyer. Why did you stop us? I wasn't speeding."

"You know this woman?" The officer asked, ignoring the cabbie's question.

"No, sir. She's just a passenger."

"Did you know you were escorting a criminal fleeing a crime scene?"

"No, sir." The cab driver knew to keep his answers brief.

"Didn't you suspect anything? Did you see money falling out of her pants, stuffed in her purse?"

"Yes, I saw that. Assumed she earned it spreading her legs."

"She's a prostitute?" Brennan jotted notes. "Where did you pick her up?"

"A taxi brought her to Harrisburg. The driver said she came from Carlisle, Locust Street, I think."

"Do you know who resides there?"

"Madam Bessie Jones and two prostitutes."

"Can you identify them?"

"No. Uh, said her name was Melissa."

"Did you know the deceased?"

"Deceased? Who's dead?" The cabbie's voice climbed higher.

"Madam Bessie Jones was murdered this morning. Did you know the deceased?" he repeated.

"Heard of her. That's mighty sad." Frown lines creased his forehead. "But it has nothing to do with me."

"I need your name, address, phone number, and a complete account of your activities and movements for the evening of

Back side of prison where Schneider climbed the fence to escape.

September thirtieth through the morning of October first." Brennan slapped a legal pad and pencil down on the table.

"Then I'm not bein' arrested?" Etnoyer asked.

"No, but you're coming to the Carlisle station for a formal interview."

The cabbie bent over the pad, tracing his movements.

Brennan waited until Schneider was processed. When backup arrived, he put her in his cruiser's back seat again and drove to the Cumberland County jail. "You'll be arraigned and charged with murder tomorrow."

They took her possessions, processed her, and led her to a cell wearing her clothes. Jittery and quaking, she dropped to the cot and buried her head in her clammy hands. She wiped them on her slacks. Nausea returned; her stomach cramped; perspiration dripped down her temple. "I can't stay here." Having never been arrested before, she smoked, she paced, she worried.

No family member claimed Madam Jones's body. After the viewing and a brief ceremony at the Ewing Brothers Funeral Home, a kind backhoe driver laid Madam Bessie Jane Jones to rest beside her mother, Cora Andrews, and her brother, William Ahl, in the Union Cemetery on October 2, 1972.[59]

CHAPTER 22

THE PRELIMINARY HEARING

Tuesday, October 24, 1972: District Justice Meade Lyons' Office[60]*

In the Commonwealth versus Georgia Schneider case, the participants included the judge, District Attorney Harold Sheely, the defendant's counselor, Herbert Goldstein, and Georgia Schneider. The Prosecution's star witness, Cassandra Jackson, sat at the D.A. table.

The D.A. produced seven witnesses; the first, Chief Deputy Coroner Dr. Robert McConaghie, the Carlisle Hospital pathologist who conducted the autopsy on Madam Jones. He testified that the cause of death came from "blood loss from the stab wound of the pulmonary artery: the artery that was cut is one of the primary vessels coming out of the heart. It is about an inch or an inch and a half right above the heart . . . [I]t is considered part of the heart."

"Did you determine the time of death?"

"Five-thirty A.M. I pronounced her dead at 7:40 A.M." He stated that Jones had been bound and gagged postmortem, but "I'm not one hundred percent certain of this."

Sheely asked about the condition of the body, establishing that the madam was overweight. McConaghie maintained that otherwise, the body's organs were in good condition.

* The Preliminary Hearing." *Notes of Testimony, Commonwealth of Pennsylvania vs. Georgia Schneider.* 24 October 1972: title pg. All subsequent quotations from this chapter use this source. (The transcript misspelled Schneider as "Schnider," which I corrected.)

The second witness, John Bubb, Yellow Cab Lines taxi driver, stated that he'd picked up Cassandra Jackson at the Star Lite Motel on Route 11, dropped his two other passengers off, then took Jackson to 20 East Locust. He summarized his movements the night of the murder.

"Sandy rang the bell, then we asked this girl on the street if she wanted a cab, and she said just wait a minute, and they both rang the bell, but the door was locked, and they couldn't get in." So, he returned Jackson to the motel and drove the other girl (Georgia Schneider) to Harrisburg after refusing to take her to Pittsburgh. "I'[d] been out here fifteen hours, and I didn't think I could stand to make that trip. We proceeded to Harrisburg, but she asked me to drive slowly(sic) and leave the light on because she wanted to count the money." By the time they crossed the South Bridge, Schneider told him to turn off the dome light so "she could hide the money . . . in her panties."

Next, D.A. Sheely questioned Art Etnoyer, the Penn Harris taxi driver who was driving the murder suspect from Harrisburg to Pittsburgh when stopped by Trooper Michael Brennan. He testified that he grew angry because the police wouldn't tell him why they stopped the cab. "[They said] "Put your hands on the roof [of the car], and they frisked me." At the Newville substation, he demanded a reason for the detention. An officer emptied a brown bag full of money. Etnoyer said, "Robbery?"

The officer said, "That girl just killed a woman in Carlisle."

When the defense counselor cross-examined him, the taxi driver revealed that his passenger complained of being cold and bruised from falling down the stairs. He then stated, "She was awful white in the face and had these scratches I could see." His fingers stretched across his abdomen.

The D.A. then called Pennsylvania State Trooper Michael Brennan to the stand. He confirmed Etnoyer's account of events on the morning of October 1, 1972. Sheely asked what the trooper did when he stopped the cab.

Brennan recounted, "I was at the front of the vehicle; two officers to the back, Corporal George Kaminsky and Trooper Ronald Garcia. We removed the defendant and Mr. Etnoyer from the vehicle . . . Trooper Andrew Kornova and I advised the defendant of her rights and then took her to the Newville sub-station." He then reported that Schneider had $2879.07 on her person.

"What did she say concerning the money or anything else?" Sheely asked.

"I asked her where she got the money, but she refused to say, then later . . . she said she worked her ass off for it."

Then the Carlisle Police Department took custody of the defendant Georgia Ann Schneider.

Cassandra (Sandy) Jones, called Sally in court, took the witness stand next. She testified that she locked the back door at East Locust but left the front unlocked that evening, leaving Bessie's to go to the Star Lite Motel to meet a man. According to her, Schneider and Madam Jones were the only occupants in the house. Upon Sally's return, she saw the defendant near Western Auto.

Sheely asked, "Did she get in the cab with you?"

Returning to 20 East Locust, "She ran back to the house and told me she robbed her [Jones], so I ran up to the front door to go untie her, you know, and the door was locked."

Jackson claimed that Schneider said to call an ambulance because she had to use a knife "because Bessie pulled a gun on her. Then I went [back] to the motel and called this man in New Kensington and asked him what I should do, and he told me to call the police, so I called the police." She admitted knowing Georgia but not well and claimed she hadn't worked with her, even though both had come from New Kensington. Later Jackson said she knew the defendant as a friend, so she contradicted herself on the stand—a credibility issue.

Some of her answers to the defense's questions sounded mud-
dled; she evaded questions about her salary but finally admitted
a girl could make a thousand dollars a month at Bessie's, said
Bessie was an 'alright' employee, not too strict.

Schneider, on cross, testified that she had never seen a gun
at the residence and claimed that Jackson was lying about the
night's events. The defendant claimed she hid in her attic room,
hearing footsteps pounding up and down the stairs. Doors slamming. She claimed Jones was mean to the prostitutes.

Carlisle Detective Robert Warner testified his findings when
he entered the East Locust Street domicile: Jones's body was lying
across her mattress. After taking photographs, he removed the gag
washcloth from her mouth, cut the silk stockings from her wrists,
and felt for a pulse but found none. He then called the coroner
and the station for additional officers to assist the investigation.

The disheveled bedroom closet door gaped open with clothes
both on the over-the-door hanger, stacked on the bedside chair
with a church booklet, paper trash piled in a box. A bottle of
Listerine, Lysol, Vicks, and a can of Sterno huddled on a narrow
dresser with a scoop in a round washbasin to the right. They
found the lock to the cedar chest in another part of the room. A
shawl was draped over the left corner of the mirror. A paper bag
sat beside the bed.

Finally, the D.A. called Corporeal Roosevelt Wilson to testify that he found the murder weapon, a switchblade knife, in
the backyard "maybe four or five feet from a . . . tree; there is a
sidewalk where the path goes on back." After the photographer
snapped pictures of the weapon, they turned it over and observed
blood on it.

Judge Lyons concludes, "The Court finds the Commonwealth
has proven a *prima facia* case, and we bind the defendant over for
the next Term of Court."

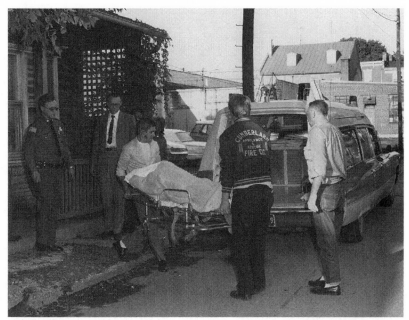

Removing Bessie's body from the house. (Courtesy of the Cumberland County Historical Society.)

Murder weapon. (Courtesy of the Cumberland County Historical Society.)

CHAPTER 23

THE TRIAL

The trial convened on February 11, 1973, with Judge Dale Shughart presiding. The defendant, Georgia A. Schneider, sat with her attorney, Herbert Goldstein; the District Attorney Harold Sheely and Cassandra Jackson sat at the prosecution's table. Although no complete transcript of the trial exists because Schneider was acquitted, the book *Bessie's House* contains a partial record of questions and answers of both prosecution and defense witnesses.

Paul Zdinak provides highlights of the trial, which parallel the preliminary hearing to some extent but with the prosecution calling more witnesses, including State Police Criminalist Harold Freed, who remarked that it wasn't his job to test for fingerprints when asked if he had.[61]

Detective Warner testified his men tested for prints and found three partials but not enough to identify the assailant. He described his discovery of the body, removing the rag from her mouth, cutting her wrist restraints, and feeling for a pulse—[but found] none.[62] "She hadn't gone to bed because she was still wearing her false teeth."

Corporeal Roosevelt Wilson retold his finding the knife in the back yard at 20 East Locust, photographing it and discovering Bessie's blood on it. Defense Counselor Goldstein cross-examined

Chief Coroner Dr. Robert McConaghie about Jones's bound wrists during the preliminary hearing, questioning whether "the victim was bound and gagged prior to or after the murder. The coroner expressed his view that she'd been tied postmortem but couldn't be one hundred percent certain. Then he changed his mind, saying during the trial that Jones was most likely tied and gagged before she died."[63]

The defense counselor later explained the significance of whether Jones's wrists were bound pre or postmortem to the press. He said a robber would tie his victim up, take the money and run; a killer would not.

(Unless the assailant wanted it to look like a robbery gone sideways).

The D.A. called the cab drivers to the stand, asking them to summarize their movements the night of the murder. Both reported the same actions they recounted during the preliminary hearing.

The prosecution's star witness, Cassandra Jackson (called Sally during the trial and Sandy elsewhere), told the jury that Schneider killed Jones, that she saw the switchblade on the defendant's bed before the killing. And afterward, waiting by the Western Auto, a pale Schneider asked for a cab ride but then returned to the scene of the crime once Jackson called the police from the Star Lite Motel.

The defense had one witness: Georgia Ann Schneider, a risky move, since she didn't have to take the stand. In the witness chair, she told a different story—that Sally warned her to stay in her room, that men were coming to rob Bessie. She said Sally left, but the defendant claimed she cowered in her room, hearing noises—thumping up and down the stairs, doors slamming. She ventured down to the second floor to discover Jones was dead, lying across her bed. She tried to call an ambulance, but the house phone was dead. Schneider ran. She held steadfast to her story, claiming that Sally lied. Goldstein rested his case.

On the morning of the third day, the D.A. requested to reopen the trial over Defense's strenuous objections. Judge Shughart agreed with Sheely. D.A. Sheely called 'Steve' (Cecil Smith) the mysterious third person involved in the prostitutes' movements during the wee hours of October 1, 1972. His story supported Jackson's version of events. He claimed he rode while a friend drove the defendant from New Kensington to deliver Georgia to the bordello, claiming she was high. "We stopped to get some coffee to try to straighten her out. We drove to Bessie's house. I said she was too high to come in . . . I said it was whiskey. Bessie said, let her come in and sleep it off."[64]

The defense counselor crossed, attacking the man's credibility because the witness had spent time in prison for murder. After the Judge dismissed Smith, Goldstein recalled Schneider to refute his testimony; she reported that Smith ran a brothel in New Kensington and insisted that he drove her from Harrisburg to Carlisle.

Both sides rested again.

The judge instructed the jury on the defendant's charges: robbery and homicide, voluntary manslaughter, second-degree robbery, robbery, or first-degree murder with life imprisonment.

Three hours later, the jury reentered the courtroom with a verdict of not guilty of robbery or homicide but guilty of an aborted prison escape.

Goldstein seemed relieved and pleased, Schneider and her mother jubilant with tears. The Schneiders left Carlisle for their home in a Pittsburgh suburb until Georgia's sentencing.[65]

On March 20, 1973, Schneider returned to Carlisle. Judge Shughart sentenced Schneider for prison breach while she was incarcerated for Madam Bessie Jones's murder. Schneider "climbed a wire fence in the prison exercise yard but was captured moments later," claiming she did it for her babies.[66] The defense counselor said his client was anxious, and the defendant told the court that she was scared. The prison guard left the back door open for a blowjob.

However, the Judge held firm. "If you had stayed where you belonged, you wouldn't be here now. The court sentences you to no less than one year and no more than four. We consider prison breach a serious matter."[67]

One year later, *The Sentinel* reported that Muncy State Prison for Women had granted Schneider a four-day furlough, but she failed to return, according to prison superintendent James Murphy.[68]

Six months later, Schneider turned up in a Pittsburgh hospital ER room after a john had beat her severely; state police escorted her to Lycoming County Court, where the judge sentenced her on September 27, 1973, for "absconding from Muncy." Two years later, on March 5, 1975, author Paul Zdinak saw Schneider, a brunette thirty pounds lighter, at the Harrisburg International Airport, on her way to Florida.[69] Schneider died in Florida in October of 2012.

CHAPTER 24

AFTERWORD

Madam Bessie Jane Jones's case remains open. An unsolved murder puzzles the mind because too many threads are left dangling. Questions persist. Where to start?

Consider the defense counselor's argument that Georgia Ann Schneider was not strong enough to plunge the knife into her employer three times. Yet with adrenalin running high, a frustrated, angry, and desperate woman would have had the force and energy to wield the murder weapon. Also, she and Jones were allegedly alone in the house at the time of the murder.

What if the killer had an accomplice? Two other people admitted to being on the premises the morning of October 1, 1972: Cassandra Jackson and Cecil Smith ('Steve' from New Kensington). Jackson testified against Schneider, but the defendant claimed the other prostitute had warned her that a robbery was imminent in the wee hours of September 30. "Stay in your room until it's over." One of the girls was lying. Another scenario: Jackson and Smith could have robbed and killed Jones, then lit out for the Star Lite Motel. They signed the motel ledger, as Mr. and Mrs. _____, so they had an alibi for the time of the murder. Smith was last seen walking along Route 11 around five A.M.

But Smith testified that he'd known Bessie since 1948—nearly twenty-five years; they were friends. Why would he kill a paying client unless the Madam had been withholding or shorting the syndicate's cut of the business for supplying and transporting the prostitutes? Others claim Jones was an independent woman. "She would not have tolerated a syndicate like the one Goldstein described trying to muscle in on her business."[70]

The defense counselor also said no blood was found on Schneider's person or her clothing, which would have been nearly impossible had she killed the madam. What if she had been wearing gloves? Or it's also possible that Jones's three layers of clothing (slip, nightgown, and robe) absorbed the blood, preventing spatters, as crime scene photos indicate.

And the switchblade found in the backyard with Rolaids paper? True, that's the act of an amateur or a desperate person. And Schneider was desperate: she said she needed another thousand to go home to Pittsburgh to have her baby (A girl she delivered in Muncy prison; officials turned the baby over to the child welfare agency). She also knew the phone was dead; that's a professional delaying tactic, someone who planned ahead.

According to his daughter, Detective Robert Warner was haunted by this case. He'd checked the body for a pulse, withdrew the gag, and cut the stockings from Jones's wrists. He investigated the crime scene and had his men search the house and grounds and dust for fingerprints. Bagged and tagged the evidence, including Jones's clothing. Interviewed the neighbors. Followed protocol. Did they miss anything? Did a neighbor fail to step forward, or had everyone been sleeping? Or had the Black community remained silent?

The coroner, Dr. Robert McConhagie, who completed the autopsy, wasn't sure that gagging and tying the victim occurred before or after she was murdered. Why? That gave the defense an opening to argue the different behaviors between a robber (who would tie a victim) and a killer (who wouldn't). That indecision laid an avenue to reasonable doubt and room for an appeal if needed. Also, did he check the victim's fingernails? The cab driver noticed scratches and bruises on Schneider's abdomen that fateful morning—a sure indication of a fight.

And what about the state troopers who apprehended the only suspect attempting to flee? Why flee if you're innocent?

Schneider had also worn the same clothes for days—a blouse or light sweater and dungarees. The cabbie had testified she'd also worn a brown coat. Shouldn't she have surrendered her clothing as evidence immediately upon being arrested? Or upon arriving at the Carlisle police station or the Cumberland County Jail? That's standard procedure.

Then there's the question of a gun that was never found on the 20 East Locust Street premises. Jackson claimed Schneider said she had to use a knife on Jones because the Madam pulled a gun on her. But in her sworn testimony, Schneider said she had never seen a gun at Bessie's—another contradiction in the prostitutes' testimonies. No gun was found on the premises.

Probably the most troubling facts: The preference and receipt books with 1600 clients' favorite sex acts listed from 1947 to 1972 were in the suspect's possession. Georgia grabbed them before she left as a bargaining tool if she were arrested, but her bags were not searched; she turned Bessie's books over to her lawyer, who told D.A. Harold Sheely that they existed. Sheely didn't want to see them, said they were not relevant to the case. How could he know that? They likely contained a list of suspects but were never examined. According to Herbert Goldstein, he later took them to the Harrisburg incinerator[71] and destroyed them. The Carlisle Sentinel reported on June 28, 1990, that Schneider gave Madam Jones's books to her defense lawyer, who claimed he kept quiet "to protect the people involved and their families from 'unnecessary embarrassment.'"[72] In journalist Wallace McKelvey's

"Mystery of the Carlisle Madam: the unsolved murder is a web of sex, politics, and racism," Goldstein stated, "Sometimes people can do the right thing in their heart and mind and still do the wrong thing."[73] He acknowledged the ethical dilemma this action posed but destroyed them anyway.

The police took possession of Schneider's $2,789 she had on her the morning after the murder, which the IRS eventually claimed for taxes as unreported revenue.

These factors and the question remain. Who killed Madam Bessie Jones? The most logical answer is probably the most accurate one. No new evidence has come to light. No new witnesses have stepped forward, but some related their stories. Most of the primary participants have died; Schneider's defense attorney reenacted his summation of the murder trial to the jury, which can be viewed on YouTube.

A tribute to Jones appeared at Carlisle's 250th-anniversary celebration—the "Bessie's House" float in the parade took second place in the history category. The John McCrea family built the float. With friends wearing period dress, they waved at the crowd along the parade route. Here's proof that some in the Carlisle community felt Madam Jones deserves a place in its history, or perhaps the McCrea gesture was a lark. "The older people were the ones who clapped, stood up, and cheered."[74] At one point along the route, one of the participants offered Police Officer Gary Schulenberger a 'nip,' (of tea), an entertaining moment.

Of course, naysayers seem relieved that Bessie's House was demolished shortly after her death and the land paved over for a parking lot. The Andrews's and Jones's brothel business expired after nearly a century in operation. Some Carlisle citizens breathed sighs; others gave thanks that the blight upon the town's good name had ended. Yet the Cumberland County Historical Society has Bessie's fur coat in its museum and a box of related articles—a testament that all history is relevant, especially her stories.

But Jones's contribution cannot be denied despite the controversy her brothel created. Yes, it was illegal, but authorities failed to shut it down, suggesting a tacit agreement between the police and the Madam. Police had other, serious crimes to solve too. And at one time, drinking in America was prohibited; speakeasies and homemade stills multiplied. Marijuana has a mixed history, too; once it was legal, then prohibited. Now medicinal marijuana has passed the bar, so to speak, and now brings relief to millions living with chronic pain.

In the histories of Carlisle that I read, Madam Jones's name is not mentioned, but her legacy has survived.

BESSIE JONES CHRONOLOGY NOTES

US Census 1860: Jane Andrews (birth 1836, Maryland) Carlisle, Pennsylvania. East Ward, Cumberland County. Children: Charles, 6; David, 2; and Cora, four months.

January 5, 1895: Four children in Cumberland County jail with Cora Andrews; court sent kids to the hospital.

April 12, 1886 and April 23, 1889: Andrews found guilty of keeping a "disorderly house." (Cress) charged, guilty. $100 fine + $1.00 court costs, "failure to abide w/rules of The Commonwealth." (*Sentinel*)

February 16, 1899: C. Andrews arrested, pled guilty to running a "bawdy house."

US 1900 Census: Cora Andrews, single: Carlisle, Pennsylvania, Ward 1, Mulberry Avenue, Cumberland County. Children: Albert Andrews (Ahl), 15; Willie, 11; Bessie Jane Andrews, 11 or 15 (born 1885 or 1889?); Marion, 5; and Vermont, 4.

January 30, 1900: Herman J. Bosler Library dedicated (East Wing).

May 15, 1902: Police raid house; C. Andrews found guilty.

1910: Thornwald mansion built—42 rooms, 8 garages, 9-hole golf course.

1917: Bessie marries William Jones, a soldier stationed at Carlisle Barracks; first listed in an arrest record of the raid on mother's "Bawdy house."

November 5, 1917: Raid by D. A. George Lloyd with state troopers (*Carlisle Evening Herald*). Charges against Cora Andrews, four 'girls' Gay Newman, Marian (sic) Andrews and Bess Jones arrested with Gettysburg soldiers with 100 bottles of beer and whiskey.

November 10, 1917: Football at Biddle Field: F&M vs. Dickinson.

November 1917: Choir rally at Shiloh Baptist Church.

November 16, 1917: Oyster Supper at Presbyterian Church. Electricity first installed in 1st Lutheran Church.

November 2, 1918 at 11:00 P.M.: Raid. Enjoying a chicken and waffle dinner; two young men, four soldiers from Gettysburg. Again, liquor was found on the premises. (*Carlisle Sentinel*)

1920s businesses: Horn's Drug Store, Woolworths, JM Shaeffer Grocer on Hanover/South Imperial Dry Goods, Bixler's Hardware, Kronenberg's & Bowman Department Stores, CCV Railroad, Carlisle Water & Gas, Hosler's Milk wagon (Chestnut horse/white blaze), etc. Streets gradually paved.

December 5, 1922: Cora Fined $50, one year in jail, tried Louis T. Figueria, Gertrude Weaver, Blanche G. Marzenello—all for keeping "bawdy house[s]." (*Sentinel*) Permits that year for 91 garages show growth auto industry.

May 14, 1923: Cora tried, defense counselor Herman Berg, State Police John Bush raided.

July 6, 1926: In a rage, Norman Morrison shoots and Frances (Stuart) Bowermaster three times, killing her. Left three daughters: Mildred, Helen, and Georgia, 3. Hyman Goldstein divorce attorney hearing 01/26 with FSB testifying husband James McBride abusive. (FSB broke off their affair).

May 29, 1934: Cora Andrews sells the property to daughter Vermont; then it's returned upon Vermont's death at 31; Bessie buys the property for $889.

September 18, 1939: BJJ arrested, plead guilty to running 'a bawdy house.' (lawyer Hymie G.)

May 9, 1941: LCB Agents arrested BJJ, "selling liquor w/o license." 2 (Cress)

March 4, 1945: Death Notice: Cora Andrews, daughter of Jane & David Andrews services Presbyterian Church, four surviving children.

1948: Carlisle school integrated.

1954 to 1958: IRS seized $86,000 BJJ deposited in a bank account for back taxes.

March 27, 1959: Charged, $1,000 bail, required health test. Beer, whiskey, quart wine.

April 14, 1959: Preliminary hearing(J.P. James D. Griest) BJJ, Joanne Ellis, 21 (blonde), and Rosemary Jones (redhead), "prostitution and assignation," "illegal sales of beer & whiskey lodged against Mrs. Jones" (*Sentinel*).

July 11, 1961: Five indictments against BJJ and 'girls' for assignation, Jones charged $3,000 bail for violating parole. IRS investigator James Mead testified Jones had $191,000 in savings from gambling and horseracing in New York. Judge Frederic Follmer one year in federal prison, five years probation (Cress WC 77). Journalists and authors report different numbers from $170,880 to $191,000 and on the amount found in the pillowcase from $48,000—$50,000.

June 27, 1963: (J.P. Frank Swigert)

July 5, 1963: BJJ charged with 'prostitution,' arrested and jailed.

September 23, 1963: Charged again, news JFK's address on joint-U.S. Russia venture into space.

March 24, 1964: Bernice Gibson (Ahl) charged (w/Frank Stackfield, Ralph Conn, and Ralph Graham—all of Locust Street) with arson, robbery at BJJ's, admitted guilt, intoxicated, took $43,600 while BJJ jailed in Muncy Women's Prison.

July 31, 1964: Feds recovers money found during house fire ($55,956) civil court in a pink pillowcase. H.G. attorney said BJJ paid $170,880 in back taxes, interest.

September 8, 1964: Edward Welsh, 28, arrested for burglary, found in an abandoned house owned by BJJ at 20 East Locust Street. Judge Dale Shughart ordered an investigation into robbery and arson at BJJ's residence. Carlisle Police Chief Edward Still. IRS confiscates nearly $50,000 in a pink pillowcase. (*Carlisle Sentinel*)

June 20, 1968: BJJ arrested again.

July 3, 1971: BJJ arrested, 15 days in jail, paroled because she had been behind bars(Muncy's State prison) since June 20, 1968.

1972: BJJ found bound and gagged, house ransacked with girls who had continued to do business there.

October 1972: BJJ found dead in her home; hands bound, gagged, and stabbed in the torso and left arm. Murder weapon found in the yard. Carlisle Police Detective Robert Warner at the crime scene. Corporal Roosevelt Wilson found a knife. Bessie's Attorney: Hyman "Hymie" Goldstein. Police chief: Frank Giordano. Dr. Robert McConaghie, autopsy. Ewing Brothers mortuary.

October 3, 1972: Georgia A. Schneider was arrested on her way to Pittsburgh in a taxi with "Steve" from New Kensington (syndicate?) with $3,000, 5 months pregnant.

October 4, 1972: BJJ's funeral sparsely attended; a volunteer agreed to dig a hole for her casket.

February 11, 1973: Judge Dale Shughart presided: Georgia Ann Schneider's murder trial begins. Defense Attorney: "Corky" Goldstein. D.A. Harold Sheely reopens cases for witness "Steve." Schneider acquitted after the 3-day trial.

ENDNOTES

1.   Zdinak, Paul. *Bessie's House.* Harrisburg, PA: Your Private Printer, 1976. Reprinted 1990. 170.

2.   "Bawdy House is Raided." *The Sentinel.* 05 November 1918.

3.   Goldstein, Herbert. "Reenactment of Closing Argument," YouTube. December 2019.

4.   "The Molly Pitcher Plea," Virginia City, NV: *Territorial Enterprise: Mark Twain's Newspaper and Virginia City News:* 08 May 1959: 1.

5.   "Lawyer Holding Bessie's Sex Book." *The Sentinel.* 28 June 1990: 1, A4.

6.   McKelvey, Wallace. "Mystery of the Carlisle Madam." *Sunday Patriot News.* December 22,2019: 1, A10–13.

7.   "The Molly Pitcher Plea," 1.

8.   "Carlisle Public Schools: Segregation to Integration." CCHS: gardnerlibrary.org February 11, 2020.

9.   Hunter, Wanda. Personal Interview with Barbara Landis. CCHS: http://www.gardnerlibrary.org/sories/Wanda Hunter. September 12, 2016.

10.   "Jane Andrews." U.S. Cennsus1860.www.familysearch.org/search collections/results?count=20gender%#3AF..id=1473181.

11.   "Cora Andrews." U.S. Census1900.www.familysearch.org/search /collections/results?count=20gender%3AF...id=1325221.

12.   "Boy Injured." *Carlisle Evening Herald*, March 16, 1894. Np.

13.   "Ad." Cora Andrews, *The Sentinel.* Np.

14.   "House of Cora Andrews Visited by Clean-up Party and Evidence Found—May Call Carlisle Men to Testify," *Carlisle Evening Herald.* 05, November 1917. www.newspapers.com/image/270460732.

15.   Ann Kramer Hoffer. *Twentieth Century Thoughts: Carlisle the Past 100 Years.* Carlisle, PA: CCSH. 2001, 56. 100–103.

[16] Dr. Alan Axelrod and Charles Phillips. *What Everyone Should Know About the 20th Century: 200 Events that Shaped the World.* Holbrook, MA: Adams Media Corporation. 1998. *83m*

[17] "House of Cora Andrews." *Carlisle Evening Herald,* 05 November 1918.

[18] Joseph D. Cress, *Crooked Carlisle.* Charleston, SC: The History Press. 2012.

[19] Axelrod and Phillips, 74.

[20] "Raid," *The Carlisle Sentinel.* 05 December 1922. Np.

[21] Hoffer, 56.

[23] "Prohibition." Axelrod and Phillips, 77.

[23] Hoffer, 55.

[24] "Kronenberg's Ad."

[25] "Andrews Charged," *The Sentinel.* 15 May 1923.

[26] Paul Hoch. *Murder in Carlisle's East End.* Charleston, SC: The History Press. 2014. 14–15.

[27] "Black Tuesday," Axelrod and Phillips, 119.

[28] See *Orphan Train* by Catherine Baker Kline whose novel depicts the harsh lives of orphans who were shipped from NYC to the rural Midwest and often treated as indentured servants.

[29] "Franklin Delano Roosevelt Launches New Deal," Axelrod and Phillips. 128

[30] "Babes in the Woods." *Carlisle Evening Sentinel.* 25 November 1934: 1.

[31] Joel Levy. *Really Useful: the origins of everyday things.* London: Firefly Books Ltd. 2002: 98.

[32] Hoffer, 123–125.

[33] "Estate Notice." *The Sentinel,* January 06, 1937. Np. The paper reported Brown's age as thirty-one, but the 1900 Census lists Vermont as four.

[34] "Richard Wright Publishes Native Son." Axelrod and Phillips, 142.

[35] Cress, *Wicked Carlisle,* 54.

[36] "PA Service Men and Women."borderieux.weebly.com/world-war II-in -Pennsylvania.htrr.

[37] See *the Code Girls: The True Story of American Women Who Secretly Broke Codes in World War II.* NY: Little, Brown, and Co. Kindle ed. 2018. Location 225. Liza Mundy describes in detail "10,000 women traveled to Washington, D.C. for code-breaking classes which served as the groundwork for cybersecurity."

[38] Tom Brokaw. *The Greatest Generation.* NY: Random House. 1998: 88.

[39] "Death Notice: Cora Andrews," *The Sentinel,* 03 March 1945. Np.

[40] "WPA See[s] Peak in Three Years," *The Patriot News,* 10 May 1945:

[41] Axelrod and Phillips, 180.

[42] See Jackson Taylor's *The Blue Orchard* for a detailed account of his grandmother's nursing career—assisting a Black doctor in Harrisburg who performed abortions.

[43] "WW II Casualties." https://borderieux.weebly.com/world-war-II-in -Pennsylvania.html.

[44] Hofer, 116.

[45] Keim, M. Personal Interview. 22 January 1920.

[46] "Trio in Raid Held for Trial." *The Sentinel.* 14 April 1959. http: //newpapers.com/image/345261001. Np.

[47] "The Molly Pitcher Plea." *Territorial Enterprise and Virginia City News: Mark Twain's newspaper.* 08 May 1959.

[48] James Brann. "Bessie Scolding," *The Patriot News,* 12 July 1961:1+ and "Sentence Lecture," *The Patriot News,* July 31, 1964: 5.

[49] Cress, 72–75.

[50] Anonymous. Personal Interview. 19 February 2020.

[51] "Sentence Court is Held Here." *The Sentinel.* 24 March 1964. http: //newspapers.com/image/344868791 Np.

[52] Ibid.

[53] Sandy Mader. "Women of Carlisle's East End," *Cumberland County History.* Summer/Winter 2003, Vol. 20, number 1–2. 43. This account reports that Jones was arrested in 1966 and sentenced to "a year in a federal penitentiary in West Virginia but released early [because]of poor health." http://newpapers.com/image/345261001. Np.

[54] Zdinak, 114.

[55] Gloria Steinem. "Address to Women of America." Youtube.com

[56] R, D. Personal Interview. 20 February 2020.

[57] Cress, 78–79.

[58] "Bessie Jones Murder; Victim's Bedroom." Photo: Shaeffer Studios.

[59] Zdinak, 114.

[60] The Preliminary Hearing." *Notes of Testimony, Commonwealth of Pennsylvania vs. Georgia Schneider.* 24 October 1972: title pg.

[61] Zdinak. 169.

62 Ibid., 177.
63 Ibid., 165.
64 Ibid, 196.
65 "Prostitute Acquitted of Murder," *The Indiana Gazette* (Indiana, PA), 16 February 16, 1973, 15. www.newspapers.com/image/13648684
66 Ibid.
67 Zdinak, 224.
68 Harold Kahn. "Georgia Schneider Missing." *The Sentinel.* 14 January 1974. www.newspapers.com/image/343827205
69 Zdinak, 231, 239.
70 McKelvey, A11.
71 Ibid.
72 Richard Reitz. "Lawyer holding Bessie's sex book. 28 June 1990: 1, A4
73 McKelvey, A11.
74 David Blymire. "Float Touts Carlisle Madam's Legacy." *The Sentinel.* 14 May 2000. www.newspapers.com/image/344581540.
75 Ibid.

SOURCES

Amerson, Carman. "Bessie's Case Still Open," *The Sentinel.* Carlisle, PA. 24 February 1990. A1–4.

Axelrod, Alan, Ph.D., and Charles Phillips. *What Everyone Should Know About the 20th Century: 200 Events that Shaped the World.* Holbrook, MA. Adams Media Corporation. 1998.

"Bawdy House is Raided." *The Carlisle Sentinel.* 05 November 1918.

Beers, Paul. "Reporter at Large." www.newspapers.com

Blymire, David. "Float Touts Carlisle Madam's Legacy." *The Sentinel.* 14 May 2000; 1, "Bessie" A4.www.newspapers.com

Brann, James. "Sentence Lecture." *The Patriot News,*

Brown, Vermont. *Obituary. The Sentinel.* 06 January 1947. www.news papers.com

"Cora Andrews," *United States Census, 1900.* https://www.familysearch. org/search/collection/results?count=20pa%22%3AF20%Brace%3A Black7collection_id1325221

Cress, Joseph David. *Blood on their Hands: Murder and Mayhem in Cumber-land County.* Charleston, SC: The History Press. 20

—. *Wicked Carlisle: The Dark Side of Cumberland Valley.* Charleston, SC: The History Press. 2012.

"Crystal Piezo Industry in Carlisle." www.tedlind.net/Crystal Industry in Carlisle.pdf

Darnell, Robert. "The Bedroom Killing of a Kindly Bordello Madam." October 1, 1972.

"Death Notice: Cora Andrews." *The Sentinel.* 04 March 1945.

Delozier, Nancy. Personal Interview. 22 February 2020.

Hoch, Paul. D. *Murder in Carlisle's East End: Unintended Consequences.* Charleston, SC: The History Press. 2014. 13–15.

Hoffer, Ann Kramer. *Twentieth Century Thoughts: Carlisle, the Past Hundred Years.* Carlisle, PA: Cumberland County Historical Society (CCHS). 2001.

Holt, Thomas. C. *Children of the Fire: A History of African Americans.* New York. Hill and Wang: 2010.

"Home of Cora Andrews Visited by Clean-up Party and Evidence is Found—"*The Carlisle Evening Herald.* 05 November 1971.

Hughes, Langston. "Mother to Son." *An Introduction to Literature.* Ed. Sylvan Barnett, et al. NY: Pearson Longman. 897.

"Hunter, Wanda." CCHS. Personal Interview w/Barbara Landis. YouTube. 11 February 2020.

Jaediker, Kermit. "Goodbye, Bessie." *Times-Tribune.* Scranton, PA: 08 October 1972.

K., Harry. Personal Interview. 22 January 1920.

King, Martin Luther, Jr. Ph.D. "Letter from Birmingham Jail," *Aims of Argument.* NY: McGraw Hill Co., Inc. 2006: 240.

Kingsboro, Pam H. Personal Interview. 30 November 2019.

"Kronenberg Department Store" ad. *The Carlisle Evening Herald,* Carlisle,19 December 1910. Pennsylvania.

"Lawyer Holding Bessie's Sex Book," *The Sentinel.* 28 June 1990. 1, A4.

Levy, Joel. *Really Useful: The Origins of Everyday Things.* Buffalo, NY: Firefly Books. 2012.

Madder, Sandy. "Women of Carlisle's East End," *Cumberland County Historical Society.* Summer/Winter 2003, Vol 2, 1–2. 42–43.

Madsen, Helen. Personal observation. 25 February 2020.

McKelvey, Wallace. "Mystery of the Carlisle Madam: the unsolved murder is a web of sex, politics, and racism." *The Sunday Patriot News.* 22 December 2019. 1, A10–12.

"The Molly Pitcher Plea." *Territorial Enterprise and Virginia City News:Mark Twain's newspaper.* 08 May 1959.

Mundy, Lisa. *The Code Girls: The Untold Story of the American Women Code Breakers of World War II.* Kindle ed. NY: Little, Brown and Co. 2018. Location 225.

Pennsylvania Jack. Pajack.com/stories/Pennsylvania/babes.html

"Police Raid House: Andrews Charged." *The Sentinel.* 30 March 1954.

"Preliminary Hearing." *Notes of Testimony: Commonwealth of Pennsylvania Vs. Georgia Schneider.* 24 October 1972.

"Prostitute Acquitted of Murder." *The Indiana Gazette.* Indiana, PA. 16 Februray1973. www.newspapers.com

Purnell, Sonia. *A Woman of No Importance: The Untold Story of the American Spy Who Helped Win WWII.* NY: Penguin Books 2020.

R., Debbie. Personal Interview. February 24, 2020.

"Sentence Court is Held Here," *The Sentinel.* March 24, 1964. www.news papers.com

Steinem, Gloria. "Address to the Women of America." Youtube.com

Taylor, Jackson. *The Blue Orchard.* New York: A Touchtone Book, Simon and Schuster. 2010.

"US Federal Court Seeks to Recover Money." *The Sentinel.* 31 July 1964.

"William A Jones." United States World War I Draft Registration Cards, 1917–1918. https://www.familysearch.org/ark:/61903/3:1:33SQ-

"Woman Arraigned in Miss Jones' Death." *The Sentinel.* 03 October 1972.

"WPB See[s] Peek in Three Years." *The Patriot.* 10 May 1945.

Zdinak, Paul. *Bessie's House.* Harrisburg, PA: Your Private Printer, 1990.

QUESTIONS FOR BOOK GROUPS

What examples of irony did you find in *Madam Bessie Jones*?

How would you assess the relationships between Cora Andrews and Bessie Jones? Between Marion and Bessie?

How does the saying, "The more things change, the more they stay the same" apply to this book?

What parallels can you see between the racial conflicts in the 1960s to 2020?

What other comparisons might observers make between Bessie's time and ours?

Why does war seem a constant theme in American history? How does it affect Carlisle?

People claim that facts don't lie. What do the facts in this book tell you?

Carlisle has a long and vivid history dating back to pre-Revolutionary war days. What does the fact of a brothel thriving in town reveal?

Throughout all my three years of research and writing, people never said an unkind word about Bessie Jones. Her lawyer claimed she was a good and decent person. How would you characterize her?

The trial of Georgia Ann Schneider received much attention at the time. Does her acquittal square with the testimonies?

ACKNOWLEDGMENTS

First, I am indebted to Nate Davis, whom I met by chance at the 2018 Carlisle Expo. He provided early Census data on Jane and David Andrews, Cora Andrews, and Bessie Jane Jones, which started the ball rolling. I owe Pat LaMarche a debt of gratitude for facilitating numerous luncheons so the assembled group could share resources and plan the Bessie J. Jones trial reenactment, giving me access to additional resources. As a journalist, she tossed me pertinent questions and suggested possible avenues of investigation.

Our Writing Critique Group—Pat, Phyllis, Sherry, and Andy—gave me valuable feedback and suggestions on organization, content, and inconsistencies in the manuscript throughout the book's journey, tracing Bessie's life and times, as well as correcting my mistakes re the historical context. I took some liberties with the chronology to fit the narration, but all the anecdotes actually occurred.

The Cumberland County Historical Society, especially librarian Rob Swartz, spent countless hours looking up news articles, photos, etc., on Bessie J. Jones and Carlisle's history. Thanks also to CCHS Photo Curator Richard Tritt for clearing Bessie's last photo for printing. Kim Laidler, manager at History on High Shop (CCHS), pointed me to individuals who remembered and shared anecdotes about Bessie. And thanks to lawyer/historian Ron Turo who supplied me with a copy of "The Preliminary Hearing of the Commonwealth of Pennsylvania vs. Georgia Schneider." And a nod to Janet Lay, who gave me Judge Shughart's wife's name.

I'm always grateful for my neighbors, family, friends, and strangers who have bought all my books—the coming-of-age debut, *Glory in the Flower* and the fact-based Carlisle Crimes Cases: *Dying for Vengeance* (my first murder mystery), *Courting Doubt and Darkness, Darkness at First Light, Had a Dying Fall, and Things Strangled,* featuring Carlisle Homicide Detectives, Erin McCoy, and Christopher Snow. My website is www.carlislecrimecases.com. I post my book news and events on my Facebook page, Carlisle Crime Cases by JM West. I hope readers feel *Madam Bessie Jones: Her Life and Times* assimilates the available information, combines the various sources and anecdotes, and clarifies some of the issues surrounding Jones's life. As my first historical book, this is a departure and an experiment for me.

As always, The Bosler Memorial Library's The Bookery supplied me with numerous history and resource books, including *What Everyone Should Know about the Twentieth Century* by Dr. Alan Axelrod and Charles Phillips, Ann K. Hofer's *Twentieth Century Thoughts, Carlisle the Past 100 Years,* and J. Cress's *Murder and Mayhem in Cumberland County* and *Wicked Carlisle, the Dark Side of the Cumberland Valley* with valuable information and insight into Madam Jones's history. Paul Hock described Francis Stuart Bowermaster's murder in *Murder in Carlisle's East End.* Also, Paul Zdinak's *Bessie's House* provided crucial background material.

The YouTube video of Corky Goldstein's summation for the defense showed how Bessie J. Jones's murder and trial affected Carlisle. The sensational story of prostitution, its secrets, and shame made a profound impression in 1972 at the time of Jones's murder and forty-seven years later, if Wallace McKelvey's 2019 article, "Mystery of the Carlisle Madam" in *The Patriot-News* is any indication.

And thanks to Terry West, my husband, for proofreading and helping me research songs. Thanks again to my sons for their computer expertise, patience, and encouragement. All errors are mine alone. I regret that three people did not respond to an interview request.

Again, I thank Sunbury Press for the opportunity to write, to tell the stories spurred by Carlisle crimes. I appreciate that the team demands my best and is willing to edit, polish, and improve my writing. To LK for editing the book and designing my book cover. To Marianne for keeping me on track and Crystal for her exacting work. Finally, thanks to all the readers who approached me at my book signings over the last nine years, asking, "Are you going to write about Bessie?" This book is a result of that question.

ABOUT THE AUTHOR

J. M. West, author of the Carlisle Crime Cases features Homicide Detectives Christopher Snow and Erin McCoy, is a Professor Emerita of English Studies at Harrisburg Area Community College, The Gettysburg Campus. She also taught at Messiah College and Shippensburg University and served as Assistant Director of the Learning Center (SU). The CCCs include *Dying for Vengeance, Courting Doubt and Darkness, Darkness*

J. K. West. (Photo by Barb Bui.)

at First Light, Had a Dying Fall*, and *Things Strangled. Glory in the Flower*, her debut novel, depicts four coeds' struggles during the turbulent sixties. See her website www.carlislecrimecases.com for details on the police procedurals by JM West on Facebook for updates and book events.

Sherry Knowlton and West co-host the "Milford House Mysteries," author interviews and writing tips on the Bookspeak Network at www.blogtalkradio.com

She and her husband live in Carlisle, Pennsylvania. They have two sons and two grandsons. They enjoy their Border Collie mix. In her spare time, West participates in a book club and writing group, and reads voraciously.

Made in the USA
Middletown, DE
15 June 2021

42316865R00094